WHY I ASSASSINATED GANDHI

NATHURAM GODSE

Compiled and Edited by
Virender Mehra

Farsight Publishers and Distributors

My life also came to an end simultaneously with the shots fired by me at Gandhiji. Since then I have been passing my days as if in trance and meditation.

I am prepared to concede that Gandhiji did undergo sufferings for the sake of the nation. I shall bow in respect to the service and to him. But even this servant of the country had no right to vivisect the country by deceiving the people.

I do not desire any mercy to be shown to me. I do not also wish that any one on my behalf should beg mercy towards me.

If devotion to one's own country amounts to a sin, I admit I have committed that sin. If it is meritorious, I humbly claim the merit thereof.

My confidence about the moral side of my action has not been shaken even by the criticism levelled against it on all sides. I have no doubt that honest writers of history will weigh my act and find the true value thereof some day in future.

Nathuram V. Godse

November 1948

Editor's Note

In the late Nineteen seventies, I came across the book 'Murder of the Mahatama and other cases from a Judge's Note Book' written by Justice G.D. Khosla. He was one of the three judges who pronounced death sentence to Nathuram Godse. It was a fascinating narrative of a judge who had interrogated the main reaction of the audience. According to him, if the audience of the day were entrusted with the task of deciding Godse's appeal, they would have brought in a verdict of not guilty by an overwhelming majority. Such was his powerful defence that he moved all the audience in his favour.

The Government of the day banned his last statement. Even in the year 2014, Prasar Bharti Board withdrew the 52 serial programme on Mahatama Gandhi, produced by Ketan Mehta and Deepa Sahi on the pretext of 'time constraints'; fearing the sympathy Godse might get. To state the play 'Me Nathuram Godse Boltoy,' the writer Pradeep Dalvi had to approach the High Court. The ban on staging the play was lifted in the year 2001. Banning or hiding the portions of history is no solution.

After having read Nathuram Godse's statement reproduced by his brother, Gopal Godse, I felt the need to compile Gopal Godse's work with Justice Khosla's narrative. I collected the photographs of all the accused and the persons related with this case to give the readers a comprehensive picture.

I am sure this book will captivate the interest of the readers who are keen to know the ugly chapter of the history, which cannot be erased.

ISBN : 81-89297-97-X

Revised Edition 2025

Published by
Farsight Publisher and Distributors
S-16, Naveen Shahdara
Delhi-110032 Phone : 22324833
e-mail : goelbooks@rediffmail.com

Laser Typesetted by
Akriti Graphics
Delhi, India

Printed by
B.K. Offset
Naveen Shahdara, Delhi-110032

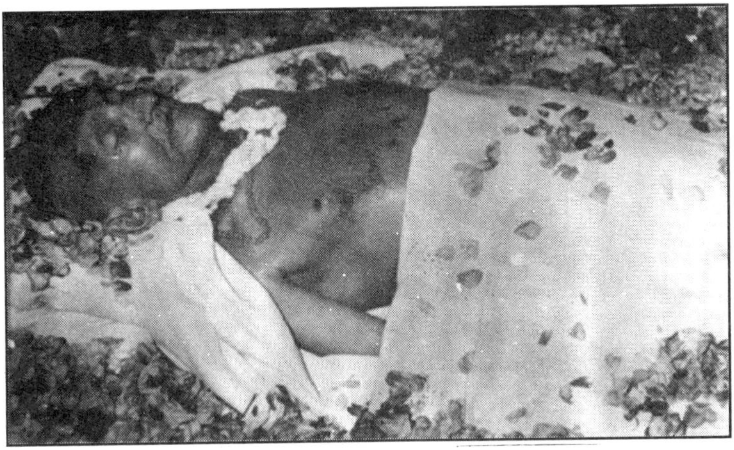

If I'm to die by the bullet of a mad man, I must do so smiling. God must be in my heart and on my lips. And if anything happens, you are not to shed a single tear."
- Gandhiji, January 28, 1948.

Mahatma Gandhi was shot in the prayer ground at 5.12 in the evening of January 30, 1948 and died fifteen minutes later.

Gandhiji left his room in Birla House for the prayer meeting a few minutes after the conclusion of his talk with Sardar Vallabhbhai Patel. As he walked up the few steps leading to the prayer mandap, a young man, aged about 35, came before Gandhiji and, bending his body forward at a distance of less than two yards, offered pranam. Gandhiji returned the salute, when the young man remarked "You are late to-day for the prayer." Gandhiji smiled and replied, "Yes, I am"; but just at that moment, the young man pulled out his revolver and rang out three shots from point-blank range, the bullets piercing the frail body of the great leader just below the heart and stomach. Immediately, Gandhiji collapsed. Thereafter, he was speechless and died at the spot.

The killer of Gandhiji and his apologists sought to justify the assassination on the following arguments:

- **Gandhiji supported the idea of a separate State for Muslims. In a sense, he was responsible for the creation of Pakistan.**
- **In spite of the Pakistani aggression in Kashmir, Gandhiji fasted to compel the government of India to release an amount of Rs.55 crores due to Pakistan.**
- **The belligerence of Muslims was a result of Gandhiji's policy of appeasement.**

The assassination of Gandhiji was a culmination of decades of systematic brain-washing. Gandhiji had become a thorn in the flesh of the hard core Hindus and in course of time, this resentment turned into a phobia. Beginning with the year 1934 over a period of 14 years on as many as five occasions, attempts were made to kill Gandhiji. The last one by Nathuram Godse on January 30, 1948, was successful. The remaining five were made in July1934, September 1944, September 1946 and on 20th January 1948. Godse was involved in two previous attempts. When the unsuccessful attempts of 1934, 1944 and 1946 were made, the proposal regarding the partition and the matter regarding release of Rs. 55 crore to Pakistan were not in existence at all. The conspiracy to do away with Gandhiji was conceived much earlier. The grounds advanced for this heinous crime are clever rationalization to hoodwink the gullible. The staging of the play entitled, "Mee Nathuram Godse Boltoy" is a clear proof of the fact that the mindset that led to Gandhiji's assassination has not disappeared from our national psyche.

At the famous Red Fort trial, in Delhi, on 8.11.1948 the special Court judge asked Nathuram, what he had to say with regard to the prosecution case against him. Nathuram Godse, made a detailed statement in his reply. It is this statement of his before the Court, that is here-with presented.

There was a ban on the publication of his statement, and this had a peculiar background. Shri C.K. Daphtary as the

Chief Prosecutor, requested the Court not to allow the accused Nathuram Godse to read the statement that he had prepared and submit the explanation to the specific charges framed against him. This request was with a purpose. The sleuths of the prosecution had figured in advance that while confessing to the charge of assassination, Nathuram wanted to dig out and depose all commissions and omissions, promises and deceits, not of Gandhi alone but also of the ruling party, which he was going to put forward as the motive behind his act and thereby make the truth public through the process of the court, and this is what the prosecution wanted to halt in the beginning. The judge Shri Atma Charan counter questioned Shri Daphtary.

How can I stop the accused from deposing? According to the accused it might be his pleading for justifiability of his act. Or, it might be the reason for denying the charges. Show me any authority or law, if you have in support of your objection.

Shri Daphtary had to admit that he had no knowledge of such law or authority that he could cite. The Court over-ruled the objection and permitted Nathuram Godse to go on with the reading of his statement.

The press carried portions of the statement the next day. Both the intelligent class and the masses which were kept in dark came to know of the stand of Nathuram Godse. They also came to know that he had not denied the charge of assassinating Gandhiji.

Pandit Nehru was the Prime Minister of India at that time. On his directions, State after State banned the publication of the statement, in part or in full.

It may be noted at this juncture that the Government became more wise when Nathuram Godse completed his arguments before the High Court at Simla in June 1949. **No sooner the judges returned to their chambers, the Police pounced on the press-reporters, snatched their note-books and tore them to pieces. They threatened the persons of true reporting.**

People, the world over, have been curious to know about the individuals connected with Gandhi Murder episode. What sort of men they were and of what ilk? is asked.

There is a persistent demand for the publication of Nathuram Godse's statement, which he had made in the Court. This is published in English, i.e. the language it was stated before the Court.

Some writers of 'repute' have ventured on the subject. In doing so, they have distorted facts, substituted lies instead of plain facts, indulged in innuendo, malicious in nature, and made dirty insinuations in their so-called literary works. They have resorted to cheap sensationalism to pander to the mood of the readers and distort history.

That apart, the authentic statement will clear the air of misgivings and meet dishonest versions given currency to sully his image by some writers. The readers may make their own evaluation from the plain facts, the bald and bare statement. To quote Nathuram himself: *"Honest writers of history will weigh my act and find the true value thereof some day in future."*

Law gives a special kind of sanctity to 'dying declarations.' The statement of Nathuram Godse, in the circumstances in which it was made, commands itself to no less a sanctity.

This book seeks to present the statement of Nathuram Vinayak Godse at the Red Fort trial in its unabridged form. Before that an introduction to the events, details of investigations and the formation of the special court are given. The proceedings after the statement was completed, the judgment, the appeals and events till 15.11.1949 when Nathuram and Apte were executed, are presented.

–Publisher

Contents

Mahatama Gandhi was having close relations with Mountbatten and his wife Edwina

THE EVENTS

Partition of India having been conceded, on 15 August 1947, the British rule came to an end and the two Dominions, —India (truncated) and Pakistan took shape. There was large scale migration of population with untold violence, murders, looting, rape and what not. The sufferings of the refugees in general and Hindus in particular presented a sorry sight, and here every action of Gandhiji was pro-Muslim and anti-Hindu. The integration of States was yet to take place. With Nizam of Hyderabad, the things were far from smooth and Kashmir was under attack.

Sardar Vallabhbhai Patel was then the Deputy Prime Minister of India. The payment of the cash balance of Rupees fifty five Crores due to Pakistan at the time of the partition of India was one of the major issues under discussion and negotiations with Pakistan. The issue was inevitably linked with Pakistan's aggression on Kashmir. In the statement made by Sardar Patel in the press conference on 12th January, 1948, he had put forward India's case in unequivocal terms. He said:

"We were therefore fully justified in providing against aggressive actions in regard to Kashmir by postponing the implementation of the agreement. The agreement does not bind the Government of India to any fixed date for payment. Pakistan would not be justified in any way in insisting on our paying the cash balances. I made it quite clear then that we would not agree to any payment until the Kashmir affair was settled."

Thus payment of Rupees fifty five Crores to Pakistan was sought to be withheld by Sardar Vallabhbhai Patel until the Kashmir issue was settled.

There are two ways to extinguish fire: One is to throw water on it and the other is to cut off supply of substances that feed it. Our army was trying its level best to halt the invaders in Kashmir and drive them away. This strategy in financial transactions by the Government of India (withholding the payment) was valuable, for it was necessary to keep off material likely to serve as fuel from reaching the fire. In these circumstances, decision of the then Government of India to withhold payment of Rs. 55 Crores until the Kashmir issue was settled was commendable. It was a far-sighted remedy to stop bloodshed immediately and establish peace. Two decades later, the march of the Indian army to Lahore to ward off the invasion of Pakistan on Kashmir under the guidance of Shastriji's Prime Ministership was as timely as it was commendable.

In those hectic days, Gandhiji was staying in Delhi. The high-ups in the Government of India used to meet him and discuss with him political issues. Gandhiji did not approve of this decision of the Government of India. Gandhiji felt that in blockading Pakistan in this way India was deviating from its path of Ahimsa. On 12.1.1948 Gandhiji threatened the Government that unless they reversed their aforesaid decision and pay the money to Pakistan, he would go on hunger strike. A portion of Gandhiji's sermon delivered on the 12th of January, 1948, that he had tried to persuade the Government of India to revoke this decision, but had failed. He said :

"But a time comes when a worshipper of Ahimsa is forced to start fast in order to express his opposition to any injustice to the society. He does so because he being a worshipper of Ahimsa has no other course open to him. Such a critical moment has come for me."

Sardar Patel's firmness must have forced Gandhiji to utter such despairing words. On the other hand, Sardar Patel did not like Gandhiji's resolve to go on hunger strike. So has echoed Maulana Azad in his book. Sardar Patel left Delhi On 13.1.1948. Gandhiji began his fast.

The net result of Gandhiji's fast was that about the 17th of January, the Government gave in and agreed to pay the money to Pakistan, thus bringing to an end Sardar Patel's policy for Kashmir.

The Government of India issued a press note (on or about 17th January 1948) which runs as follows:

'In view of the appeal made by Gandhiji to the nation the Government has decided to remove the cause of suspicion and friction between the two States which consistently with national honour and national interest, is in their power to remove.

The government makes this spontaneous gesture in the earnest hope that it will help in producing an atmosphere of goodwill for which Gandhiji is suffering crucifixion of the flesh and thereby lead this great servant of the nation to end his fast and add still further to his unparalleled services to India.

The Government has decided to implement immediately the financial agreement with Pakistan in regard to cash balances.'

With all this overflowing generosity and goodwill from the Indian Government the Pakistani heart did not melt. The Kashmir problem continued.

Nathuram Vinayak Godse and Narayan Dattatraya Apte were running a daily by the name of 'Hindu Rashtra', which earlier was 'Agrani' but now was in a new garb. Even prior to 15 August, 1947, the foreboding signs of the creation of a Muslim State, founded on communal principle on the very Indian soil were becoming clear every passing day. The editorials of this newspaper began to be more and more pungent and critical. There were even orders of forfeiture of the two security deposits of Rs. 3,000/- each.

On seeing the news item on the teleprinter on 12th January, 1948, that Gandhiji was to start his fast, it became clear to Nathuram Godse that this act was contemplated to bring pressure on the Government of India to reverse their decision of withholding the payment of fifty-five crores of rupees. By that time his embittered feelings about Gandhiji and his continued anti-Hindu role reached its point of culmination. As soon as he read the news item on the teleprinter about Gandhiji's fast, Nathuram must have thought that all other plans should be set aside. Care had to be taken to see that Gandhiji did not interfere with the democratic working of the Government. For that sake the task of assassinating Gandhiji should be taken up first and his everything should be staked for it. According to Nathuram it was a matter of life and death for the nation.

On 20 January, 1948, a bomb had exploded at Gandhiji's evening prayer near the prayer ground. Madan Lal Pahwa was apprehended on the spot. He was one of the Hindu sufferers of partition. The police got information that Madan Lal had other accomplices too in the plot, and their plan did not work and his co-conspirators must have fled. As a consequence, the Government reinforced the police force and security measures at the Birla House. The police spread a net all over India, to apprehend others.

The police could however make no progress in apprehending others within the next ten days.

On 30.1.1948, at five past five in the evening, when Gandhiji, accompanied by a two young girls, was coming to the prayer ground, in the compound of Birla House, Nathuram Vinayak Godse fired three shots at point blank range. Gandhiji with a faint 'ah', possibly as a reflex action of muscles, fell to the ground. He went unconscious instantaneously and breathed his last about twenty minutes later. Nathuram after firing shots raised his hand with the gun and called for the police. He voluntarily surrendered to the authorities.

Nathuram Godse was fully aware that after the assassination of Gandhiji at his hands political powers of the day would append to him all sorts of attributes; such as fanatic, maniac, lunatic and many others. That is why he earnestly wished to be officially recorded by the concerned authorities at the very moment that he suffered from no such malady, mental or physical. That his mental state did not conform to any definition of mental distortion, disease or aberration. The request made by Nathuram to the doctor who was brought to examine him soon after his arrest following the assassination of Gandhiji was:

Doctor, kindly examine me thoroughly and record faithfully if my pulse and heart are working normally.

The doctor did likewise and declared that his heart and pulse beat quite normally.

After his surrender and arrest, Nathuram was kept for some time in the police lock-up at Tughlaq Road and thereafter he was taken to the police custody at Parliament Street. Along with the authorities some other people also came to have a look at him. Nathuram was pacing to and fro in the lock-up, but some times he stood near the bars.

Catching the sight of one individual he stood near the bars, and asked him :

You are Shri Devadas Gandhi, I suppose.

Yes, but how did you recognise me?

was the counter-question by that individual. He had perhaps come there expecting to find some horrid-looking, blood-thirsty monster, without a trace of politeness. Nathuram's gentle and clear words and his self-composure were quite inconsistent with what he had expected to see.

We had gone together very recently at a press-conference. You'd gone there as the editor of The Hindustan Times.

And You?

I am Nathuram Vinayak Godse, the editor of a daily 'Hindu Rashtra'. I too was present there. Today you have lost your father I am the cause of that tragedy. I am very much grieved at the bereavement that has befallen on you and the rest of your family. Kindly believe me. I was not prompted to do this with any sort of personal hatred, or any grudge or with any evil intention towards you.

Seeing that a man, the blood-stains on whose death-causing hands had not yet dried up, was talking to him in such a calm and balanced way and in a manner in which a third party may speak. Shri Devadas Gandhi's curiosity was aroused. There was nothing unnatural, if he were to feel intense contempt for his father's assassin. If he had that feeling, at least he did not show it then, and brushing aside for a moment his personal sorrow for his father's demise, asked Nathuram, Then, why did you do it ?' Nathuram replied, The reason is purely political and political alone. Would you listen to me for half an hour or so? Kindly ask for the officer's permission. As you are an editor you will soon understand the background.' The police did not allow further discussion.

THE POLICE INVESTIGATION;

The Arrests and The Special Court

Nathuram Godse had surrendered to the Delhi Police on the spot. The enquiry started that very night. As long as Nathuram's name was not disclosed people were making wild guesses. The refugees became restless, lest the assassin of Gandhiji might turn out to be one of them! Subsequently Nathuram's name was disclosed and it was clear that he was neither a Punjabi, nor a Bengali, nor a Sindhi nor even a refugee! Joy was openly expressed in cities like Amritsar, Ambala, Calcutta, Kanpur and others.

Digamber Ramchandra Badge was arrested by the Pune Police on 31.1.1948 and later taken in their charge by the Bombay Police.

Thousands of people all over the country were arrested under Preventive Detention laws. V.D. Savarkar was also one of them also. Later, and apparently for reasons stated in the chapter dealing with Savarkar, the arrest of Savarkar was converted from one under Preventive Detention Act into one as an accused in the Gandhi Murder case.

Madan Lal Pahwa had already been arrested ten days before the assassination, at the time of bomb explosion on 20th January. He did not have anything to add to the information, he had given to the investigation relating there to.

On Monday morning, i.e. on 2.2.1948 when I (Gopal Godse) took leave of my wife and left the house I had given her a fair idea of the possibility of my being arrested any time. At that time I had set up my residence at Khadki, a suburb of Pune. On the 5th February 1948, I left Khadki for Kamshet. I got down at Kamshet and made for Uksan which was at a distance of ten miles from Kamshet. I had not covered half the distance when I saw the Police van following me. They took me in to their van.

Shankar Kistaiyya, Badge's servant walked into the C.I.D. Office, Bombay on 6.2.1948. The last persons to be arrested were Nana Apte and Karkare, who were arrested in Bombay by the Police on 13th and 14th of February, 1948. Dr. Parchure of Gwalior was arrested and kept imprisoned in the Gwalior Fort itself

On the 25th of May 1948 all of us who had been kept in the C.I.D. Office, Bombay, were taken to Delhi by plane in two batches. As Savarkar was not well on that day he was brought to Delhi next day i.e. on the 26th of May 1948 from the Arthur Road Prison.

On 27th of May 1948 we were brought to the entrance of the specially made prison in the Red Fort and it was there, we all, including Savarkar and Dr. Parchure, saw one another.

Badge had turned approver before the date fixed for next hearing. He did not sit in the dock thereafter

In 1947, the Bombay Legislature passed a law, known as the Bombay Public Security Measures Act (Act IV of 1947), with the provisions, such as the appointment of a special Court, the appointment of a single judge with the powers to record, setting aside the usual procedure of preparing the charge-sheets and charges, to pronounce death sentence or the sentence of transportation for life, for the attempt to murder, to conduct the work of prosecution promptly and continuously, to reduce the period of appeal from 60 days to 15 days. This Act was made applicable to Delhi as well in 1948 so far as this prosecution was concerned.

From the murky, musty atmosphere of solitude we had come into open environment of the Court. It was 27th of May 1948 and the time was half-past nine in the morning. The atmosphere in the Court was still more reliving. The Court-room was a hall, admeasuring about a hundred feet in length and twenty-two feet in width, and was located on the first floor.

The Gandhi assassination case had assumed as much importance and gravity as the actual incident of the assassination. One of the reasons for this was that the Government had implicated in this conspiracy no less a person than the internationally well-known Swantantrya-Veer Savarkar himself. Savarkar, who for the major part of his life had organised secret societies for the liberation of India from foreign bondage in and out of India. He, who endured incomparable hardships, harassment and torture in that attempt; who rekindled the flame of self-respect amongst the Hindus by propounding and propagating the political philosophy for the Hindu Nation.

At 10 A.M., the Registrar of the Court announced the arrival of the Judge. The Photographers focused their cameras on the Judge and the dazzling flash lights glowed and flickered off one after another. Shri C.K. Daphtary stood up, saluted the judge and read out the charge-sheet against the accused and submitted it to the Court.

The Court ordered the summaries of the statements of the witnesses to be given to the defence counsels by the 2nd June 1948. The Court would sit again on the 3rd June 1948. After returning from the Court, we arranged our luggage.

As was decided earlier, the Prosecution supplied Shri A narao Bhopatkar with a copy of the statements of the witnesses. Although Shri Bhopatkar was pleading for Savarkar, he was entrusted the charge with overall guidance of the defence in general. Shri Ganpat Rai and Shri Jamnadas Mehta and other pleaders helped the other accused, besides their work for the defence of Savarkar.

The Court framed the charges against us the accused on the 22nd June 1948. The Judge asked each of the accused if he accepted the charges to be true. We denied the charges. Madan Lal submitted a written statement while denying the charges, in which he said:

'I deny that there was ever any conspiracy to do any harm whatever to Mahatma Gandhi or that I was involved in such conspiracy. The incident of 20th January 1948 was meant only to demonstrate the widespread dissatisfaction in the country with the pro-Muslim policy and action which Gandhiji was advocating in those days. It was nothing more.'

While denying the charges, Dr. Parchure said that he was the resident of Gwalior. The State of Gwalior had not acceded to the Union Government of India by then. The Government of India had not issued the extradition warrant against Dr. Parchure before he was taken into its custody.

Shri C.K. Daphtary, the Chief Public Prosecutor, opened the case and at the end of the day he requested the Court to visit the site of the incident. Nathuram declined. Apte, Karkare, Madan Lal and Gopal showed their desire to visit the spot, while Shankar Kistaiyya, Dr. Parchure and Savarkar said they were not interested. The visit was fixed at 10 A.M. on the 24th June 1948.

We were observing the, spot with a view to answer the statements, the Prosecutors might make in order to prove the charge they had levelled against us. But that was a minor consideration with us, as our lawyers were more competent. The thought, that we were very thickly connected with the background of the incident because of which that place had suddenly sprung into the limelight, was uppermost in our minds.

That was a spot where a chapter of Indian history came to an end. Because it was a place where the life of one who had dominated for decades the political life of the Indian nation had ended. And again it was a place which made it imperative for others with peaceful disposition to stake their lives. It was a place where a society besmeared all over with blood as a consequence of the false notions of the Hindu-Muslim unity went to show Gandhiji their open gashcs and the deep-rooted sorrow of their hearts and to tell him the harrowing tales of the thousands of victims of the Partition. That was a place where they expected their bleeding wounds to find a tongue strong enough to voice their unbearable affliction to the world. But, it was also a place, where the selfish sycophants gathered around Gandhiji and gave him the impression that his policy of non-violence was completely successful and that the political revolution had been brought about without even a drop of blood being shed. This was the same spot where Gandhiji assured Maulana Azad that the refugees from Pakistan who had sought shelter in India and housed in the houses of those Muslims who had left the country for their new home in Pakistan, should again be brought back. The Muslims who had left should be wooed to come back and their property be returned to them. This was the place where the fast to compel the Government to revert its decision of withholding the payment of fifty-five crores of rupees was undertaken. And lastly it was the place where the anti-Hindu policies emanated, and as it emerged in the years to come, were so conveniently adopted for selfish gains.

As we were surveying the place all this fresh history was unfolding itself before our eyes once again. This recent past did not appear to us as clear as it was made out to be, nor did it appear bloodless. We felt that the very atmosphere there was surcharged with blood, the blood of the martyrs who laid down their lives for the attainment of national freedom, the blood of the innocent victims of the inhuman atrocities committed due to the vivisection of the country. We also felt that as a natural concomitant to all this the blood of Gandhiji was lending a deepening dye to this ghastly atmosphere. And now perhaps as a culminating draught this hideous atmosphere was thirsting for the blood of at least some of us.

All this blood that was shed and that was still to be shed, I thought was the price that we paid for the national independence won so dearly. His assassination was likely to demand the sacrifice of lives of some of us, accused. While saying that Swaraj was attained without any bloodshed, was a great insult—and sadly enough who do not realise it that the blood so profusely shed was of the millions of Hindus. In fact we are surrounded by the crafty selfish politicians and their sycophants, by dinning this falsehood into our ears day in and day out.

The trial began and the prosecution commenced showing the evidence. The endeavor of the prosecution was to establish connections between the accused with one another during the period which they alleged when the conspiracy was hatched. Nathuram Godse and Narayan Apte were the editor and managing director respectively, of the daily 'Hindu Rashtra'. This fact was undisputed. The prosecution tried to prove that both of them travelled together to Bombay, Delhi and Gwalior. They further proved their stay at Marina Hotel, New Delhi between 17 January 1948 to 20 January 1948 and at the railway station retiring room at Delhi Junction on 29th and 30th January 1948.

The prosecution also alleged that Karkare, Gopal Godse, Madan Lal Pahwa, Digambar Badge and Shankar Kistatyya had gathered in the Marina Hotel on the 20 January 1948. But for this allegation on part of the prosecution there was no other evidence than that of Digambar Badge, the approver.

A witness from the Marina Hotel where Nathuram and Apte had stayed brought in their register to show the entries of Nathuram Godse and Narayan Apte under fictitious names.

A taxi driver deposed that he took Nathuram Godse, Narayan Apte, Gopal Godse and Vishnu Karkare, Digamber Badge and Shankar Kistatyya to the Birla House on the evening of 20.1.1948 and also took three of them back to Connaught Place.

The prosecution brought some witnesses against Dr. Parchure to prove that he was originally from British India, that is from that part of India which was not governed by the Princes. The prosecution wanted to establish that since Dr. Parchure belonged to British India, no extradition warrant was necessary. There was yet another point. There was no Arms Act existing in Gwalior State. Dr. Parchure could not be charged with an offence under the Arms Act if it were proved that he hailed from Gwalior; the State had not merged in the Union of India till the day in question.

In order to show that the conspiracy continued even after 20th January 1948 till the goal of assassinating Gandhiji on 30th January 1948 was reached. The prosecution brought a witness from Thane (Maharashtra) to prove a meeting between Nathuram Godse, Narayan

Nathuram Godse

> *There was no legal machinery by which [Gandhi] could be brought to book... I felt that [he] should not be allowed to meet a natural death.*
> *–Naturam Godse*

Apte, Karkare and myself. A mere meeting however could not establish the existence of the conspiracy.

The evidence against Veer Savarkar and his reply to the allegations has been narrated later. The Prosecution had brought as many as 149 witnesses. Their evidence ran into 720 pages.

Then on 8.11.1948, it was the turn of the accused. Accused No. 1 was Nathuram Vinayak Godse. He desired to make a detailed statement. Shri C.K. Daphtary objected to the making-of any lengthy statement. The Special Judge overruled the objection and said: "Go on, make your statement." And, began Nathuram Godse with the words that resounded.

MAY IT PLEASE YOUR HONOUR:

PART-I

Answer to the Charge-Sheet

I, Nathuram Vinayak Godse, the first accused above named respectfully beg to state as under:

1. Before I make my submission as regards the various charges I respectfully submit that the charges as framed are not according to law, in as much as there is a misjoinder of charges and there ought to have been two separate trials one relating to the incident of the 20th of January 1948 and the other relating to the incident of the 30th of January 1948. The two having been mixed up together the whole trial is vitiated.

2. Without prejudice to my above submission I make my submission in respect of the various charges as framed are stated hereafter.

3. In the charge-sheet preferred against the accused, at number of counts it has been stated that each of the accused individually and jointly with others has been charged with the commission of the various offences punishable under the Indian Penal Code and other statutes.

4. It appears from the charge sheet that the Prosecution takes the events that have happened on 20th January 1948 and thereafter on 30th January 1948 as one and the same or a chain of events in continuation of one and the same object culminating in the murder of Gandhiji. I therefore, wish to make it clear at the outset that the events upto 20th January 1948 are quite independent and have no connection whatsoever with what happened thereafter and on 30th January 1948.

5. The first and the foremost amongst the said charges is the charge of conspiracy amongst the accused to murder Gandhiji. I shall therefore first deal with the same. I say that there was no conspiracy of any kind whatsoever amongst the accused to commit any of the offences mentioned in the charge-sheet. I may also state here that I have not abetted any of the other accused in the commission of the alleged offences.

6. I say that the evidence led by the Prosecution in this regard does not establish and prove that there was any conspiracy whatsoever. The only witness who deposes about the alleged conspiracy is Digambar R. Badge (Prosecution Witness 57). He is a totally unreliable witness as will be proved Your Honour by my counsel when he explains the case and deals with the evidence of this witness - P.W.57.

7. As regards the charge of collecting and transporting arms and ammunition without licence, and abetment thereof on 20th January 1948, I say that I deny the said charge and say that I neither carried or transported gun-cotton slabs, hand-grenades, detonators, wicks, pistols, or revolvers and cartridges etc. as alleged. Nor did I have under my control any of such arms and/or ammunition, nor did I abet and aid any of the accused to do so, either before or on or about to 20th January 1948 or any other date. I deny therefore that I contravened any of the provisions of the Indian Arms Act or the Indian Explosives Substances Act and that I committed any offence punishable under the said Acts.

8. The main evidence in regard to this charge is the evidence of Digambar R. Badge (P.W.57), but as stated in paragraph 6 above, he is a totally unreliable witness. This witness Badge (P.W.57), is known to me. He hardly came

to me, nor have I ever visited his place of residence since several years. His statement that he came to the Hindu Rashtra Office on 10th January 1948, being brought there by Apte, the accused No. 2, is totally false and I deny that the said Badge saw me at the Hindu Rashtra Office or any other place on that day. Or that in my presence Apte and he had any talk between themselves about gun-cotton slabs, hand-grenades, etc. and about the delivery thereof at Bombay, as alleged by the said Badge. His statement that Apte asked me to come out of the room and that Apte told me to hand over the hand grenades etc. and that one work was over is totally false. This is a story got up by Badge to implicate me and others into the alleged conspiracy. I further say that I neither saw nor met Badge on 14th January 1948 at Dadar, either alone or in the company of Apte. I did not even know that Badge had come to Bombay on that day.

9. I further deny that I had in my possession or under my control, while at Delhi, or abetted any one to have and possess on 20th January 1948, any arms or ammunition as stated in the charge-sheet under the heading *'Secondly'* paragraphs B(1) and (2).

Here also the evidence to support this charge is of Badge alone and I say that he has given false evidence to save his own skin, on that condition alone, he could secure the pardon promised and granted to him.

10. As regards the charge under the heading *'Thirdly'*, I say that I deny the said charge and the abetment thereof as stated in several paragraphs A(1) and (2), and B(1) and (2).

11. As regards the charge under the heading *'Fourthly'* paragraph 2; I deny that I abetted Madanlal K. Pahwa either myself alone or along with others to explode a gun-cotton slab on 20th January 1948 at Birla House, I say

that there is no evidence to substantiate this charge and whatever little evidence there may be, can hardly connect me with the explosion of the gun-cotton slab.

12. As regards the charge of abetment in the attempt to commit the murder of Mahatma Gandhi under the heading *'Fifthly'* in the charge sheet, I deny the said charge and say I had no connection either directly or indirectly with Madanlal K. Pahwa or any other person whatsoever. I further say that there is no evidence whatsoever to support this charge.

13. As regards the charge under the heading *'Sixthly'* in the charge-sheet as to paragraphs (A)(1) and (2) thereof, I say that I have not imported or brought unlicensed pistol and ammunition with the assistance of Narayan D. Apte. I also deny that Dr. Dattatraya S. Parchure and Narayan D. Apte procured the said pistol, or any one of them individually or jointly; abetted me or themselves to each other in procuration of the said pistol and the ammunition. I further say that the evidence produced by Prosecution in that behalf is not reliable. Without prejudice to the above, I further say that even if the acts mentioned in these paragraphs A(1) and (2) may have been committed, this Honourable Court has no jurisdiction to take any notice of them. I further say that so far as I am concerned the charge, if any, would merge under the charge in paragraph B(1) under this head.

14 As regards the charge under paragraph B(1) and (2), I admit that I had in my possession automatic pistol No. 606824 and cartridges. But I say that neither Narayan D. Apte nor Vishnu R. Karkare had anything to do with the pistol in my possession.

15. But before I pass to the charge under the heading *'Seventhly'*, it will not be out of place to explain here how I

happened to come to Delhi, and why I came to Delhi. I have never made a secret about the fact that I supported the ideology or the school which was opposed to that of Gandhiji. I firmly believed that the teachings of absolute *'Ahimsa'* as advocated by Gandhiji would ultimately result in the emasculation of the Hindu Community and thus make the community incapable of resisting the aggression or inroads of other communities especially the Muslims. To counteract this evil I resolved to enter public life and formed a group of persons who held similar views. In this Apte and myself took a leading part and as a part of propaganda started a daily newspaper 'Agrani'. I may mention here that it was not so much the Gandhian *'Ahimsa'* teachings that were opposed by me and my group, but Gandhiji while advocating his views always showed or evinced a bias for Muslims, prejudicial and detrimental to the Hindu Community and its interests. I have fully described my point of view hereafter in detail and have quoted numerous instances which unmistakably establish how Gandhiji became responsible for a number of calamities which the Hindu Community had to suffer and undergo.

16. In my paper 'Agrani' or 'Hindu Rashtra', I always strongly criticised Gandhiji's views and his methods such as fast for achieving his object, and after Gandhiji started holding prayer meetings, we—Apte and myself—decided to stage peaceful demonstrations showing opposition. We had made such demonstrations at Panchagani, Poona, Bombay and Delhi. There was a wide gulf between the two ideologies and it became wider and wider as concessions after concessions were being made to the Muslims, either at the suggestion or connivance of Gandhiji and the Congress which was guided by Gandhiji, culminating in the partition of the Country on 15th of

August 1947. I have dealt with this point in detail hereafter. On 13th of January 1948, I learnt that Gandhiji had decided to go on fast unto death. The reason given for such fast was that he wanted an assurance from Hindu-Muslim unity in Indian Dominion. But I and many others could easily see that the real motive behind the fast was not merely the so-called Hindu-Muslim unity, but to compel the Dominion Government to pay the sum of Rs. 55 crores to Pakistan, the payment of which was emphatically refused by the Government. As an answer to this, Apte suggested the same old method to stage a strong but peaceful demonstration at the prayer meetings of Gandhiji. I consented to this half-heartedly, because I could easily see its futility. However, I agreed to join him as no alternative plan was as yet fixed in my mind. It was for this reason that N.D. Apte and myself went to Bombay on the 14th January, 1948.

17. On 15th January, 1948 we—Apte and myself—happened to go to the Hindu Sabha Office at Dadar in the morning. I happened to see Badge there. On seeing N.D. Apte and myself, Badge talked to N.D. Apte and asked him the reason of his coming to Bombay. Apte told him the reason. Badge thereupon of his own accord offered to come to Delhi and join in the demonstration, if we had no objection to his coming there. We wanted men to back us and to shout slogans and we therefore accepted his offer. We asked him as to when we could start. Badge thereupon told Apte that he had to give some stuff to Pravin Chandra Sethia. That he would do so in a day or two and would see us on the 17th January, 1948.

18. We had met Badge on 15th January, 1948 at the Hindu Sabha Office at Dadar, thereafter I met Badge on the 17th of January, 1948 in the morning.

19. The statements made by Badge about our going to Dixitji Maharaj along with him and seeing Dixitji Maharaj, about Apte having told Badge that Savarkar had entrusted Apte and myself the task of finishing Gandhiji, Pandit Jawaharlal and Surhawardy is a pure concoction and product of Badge's brain. Neither Apte nor I have ever said anything like this to Badge or any other person.

I deny categorically what the Prosecution has falsely maintained that I was guided in my action by Veer Savarkar and that, but for his complicity, I could never have acted in the way I have done. I take the strongest exception to this untrue and unjust charge and I further regard it as an insult to my intelligence and judgment. The prosecution's attempt to make out that I was a mere tool in someone else's hands is an aspersion which is far from truth. Indeed it is a perversion of it.

20. Badge's statements to the effect that I wanted to go to Poona to meet my brother Gopal Godse who had undertaken to make arrangements for procuring a revolver and bring him down to Bombay for accompanying us to Delhi, is also untrue. I had no talk with Badge when I met him on 15th January 1948 except what is stated in paragraph 17 above. Further the statement of Badge that he met me on 16th January 1948 at Poona is also false. The alleged report of my conversation with him at Poona as deposed by Badge in his evidence is also false and untrue. I was not in Poona on the 16th January 1948. It will be clear from this that it is not true that I gave him any pistol on that day for getting it exchanged for a big revolver.

21. I have already stated that we—Apte and myself—had planned to stage a strong but peaceful demonstration at Gandhiji's prayer-meeting at the earliest possible

opportunity at Delhi, and for that purpose Apte and myself were to go there. As stated in paragraph 17, Badge offered to come to Delhi to take part in the demonstration mentioned above. We felt an urgent need for taking some volunteers with us for a successful demonstration. Before we started for Delhi we started collecting money to meet the expenses for the journey and the expenses of the volunteers.

22. I emphatically deny that we saw Savarkar on the 17th January, 1948 or that Savarkar blessed us with the words *'Yashasvi Houn Ya,'* (Be successful and come). Similarly I also deny that we had any conversation with Badge or that Apte or myself uttered the words—*'Tatyaravani ase Bhavishya kele ahe ki Gandhijichi Shambhar Varshe bharali—ata apale kam nishchita honor yat kahi sanshaya nahi.'* After we met Badge on 15th January, 1948 at the Hindu Sabha Office at Dadar, we—Apte and myself—went on our business in connection with the Press.

23. Apte and myself came to Delhi by plane on the 17th of January, 1948 and we stayed at Marina Hotel. On the morning of 20th January, 1948 Badge came to the hotel and informed Apte in my presence that he and his servant Kistaiya would go to the prayer-ground in the evening with Apte just to see the scene of prayer where demonstrations would be held. When Badge came in the morning I was lying down on the bed as I was feeling unwell owing to severe headache and I told Badge that I may not be able to go to the prayer-ground as I was unwell. The statements of Badge that Apte, Gopal Godse, Karkare, Madanlal, Badge and his servant Shankar all collected at Marina Hotel. That Shankar and Badge had their meals/ there. That Gopal Godse was found repairing the revolver. That Apte, Karkare, Madanlal and Badge went to the bath-

room and were fixing the detonators, fuse-wires and primers to the gun-cotton slabs and hand-grenades or that Shankar and I were standing at the either side of the door of the room are entirely false. Badge has put in my mouth the words *'Badge, this is our last effort—the work must be accomplished—see to it that every thing is arranged properly.'* I deny that I addressed the said or similar words to Badge on that day or any other day. As stated before, Badge came to the room in the morning and informed me that he would attend the prayer-meeting in the evening. We had no meeting at all on that day in my room as stated by Badge. Gopal Godse, to my knowledge, was not even in Delhi. Nobody arranged or fixed detonators fuse-wires or primers to gun-cotton slabs or hand-grenades in the room. In fact there was no such ammunition either with me or with Apte. Badge's vivid description about the distribution of arms and ammunition amongst the party and about assumption of false names is all false. It is not necessary for me to discuss the evidence and show the falsity of these statements as my counsel will do it in his address.

24. As stated above, being unwell due to severe headache, I did not even go to the prayer-ground. Apte returned to Marina Hotel at about 6.00 p.m. and informed me that he had a view of the prayer meeting and would be in a position to stage the demonstration in a day or two. After about an hour, we heard some commotion at Gandhiji's prayer meeting due to an explosion and we further heard of an arrest, of a refugee. Apte thought it advisable to leave Delhi immediately and we left accordingly. It is not true that I met Badge at Hindu Sabha Bhavan on 20th January 1948. Several witnesses have deposed about my being at the Birla House on the 20th January, 1948. But I emphatically say that they are grossly mistaken in saying so. I submit that they are

confusing my presence with somebody else's. The identification by some of these witnesses is utterly unreliable in view of the fact that I had not been to the Birla House on that day. These witnesses have identified me as I was shown to many of them by the Police while I was kept at the Tuglak Road Police Station. Further, it was easy to identify me on account of the bandage over my head which remained up to the 12th of February 1948. The Police witnesses who have deposed, have perjured themselves and I have made complaint at the very first identification parade in respect of the Delhi witnesses held in Bombay about this.

25. After a deliberate consideration of our future plan of staging the demonstration at Delhi in the prayer-meeting of Gandhiji. I very reluctantly consented to join Mr. Apte. It was not possible to get willing and able volunteers from Bombay and Poona under the new situation. Besides all our funds were exhausted and we were not in a position to spend for the batch of volunteers from Bombay to Delhi and back. We, therefore, decided to proceed to Gwalior and see Dr. Parchure who had under him the volunteers of Hindu Rashtra Sena. It was also a more or less an economical plan to take volunteers from Gwalior to Delhi. We therefore started for Gwalior, by the night train reaching Gwalior very early morning. As it was dark at that time we halted in a Dharamshala near the Station and in the morning we saw Dr. Parchure at his residence. He was in a hurry to go to his dispensary. He asked us to see him in the afternoon. We met him at about 4 p.m. and found that he did not wish to help us, as his volunteers were busy in local affairs. Completely disappointed I asked Apte to go back to Bombay or Poona and try for volunteers there. I came back to Delhi after telling Apte that I would myself try for volunteers from

amongst the refugees. I deny categorically and with all the emphasis at my command that Mr. Apte and myself had been to Gwalior to secure a revolver or a pistol, as number of such revolvers were being offered for sale clandestinely. Having reached Delhi in great despair, I visited the refugee camps at Delhi. While moving in the camps my thoughts took a definite and final turn. By chance, I came across a refugee who was dealing in arms and he showed me the pistol. I was tempted to have it and I bought it from him. It is the same pistol which I later used in the shots I fired. On coming to the Delhi Railway Station I spent the night of the 29th thinking and re-thinking about my resolve to end the present chaos and further destruction of the Hindus. I shall now deal in detail about my relations with Veer Savarkar in political and other matters of which the prosecution has made so much.

26. Born in devotional Brahmin family, I instinctively came to revere Hindu religion, Hindu history and its culture. I had been intensely proud of Hinduism as a whole. Nevertheless as I grew up I developed a tendency to free thinking unfettered by any superstitious allegiance to any *'ism'*, political or religious. That is why I worked actively for the eradication of untouchability and the caste system based on the birth alone. I publicly joined anti-caste movements and maintained that all Hindus should be treated with equal status as to rights—social and religious, and should be high or low on their merit alone and not through the accident of birth in a particular caste or profession. I used publicly to take part in organised anti-caste dinners in which thousands of Hindus, Brahmins, Kshatriyas, Vaishyas, Chamars and Bhangis broke the caste rules and dined in the company of each other.

27. I have read the works of Dadabhai Naoroji, Vivekanand, Gokhale, Tilak along with the books on

ancient and modern history of India and some prominent countries of the world like England, France, America and Russia. Not only that, I studied tolerably well the current tenets of Socialism and Communism too. But above all I have studied very closely whatever Veer Savarkar and Gandhiji have written and spoken. As to my mind, these two ideologies have contributed more to mould the thought and action of modern India during the last fifty years or so, than any other single factor has done.

28. All this reading and thinking brought me to believe that above all it was my first duty to serve the Hinduism and the Hindu people, as a patriot and even as a humanitarian act. For, is it not true that to secure the freedom and safeguard the just interests of some thirty crores of Hindus constituted the freedom and the just interests and the well-being of one fifth of human race? This conviction led me naturally to devote myself to the new Hindu Sanghatanist ideology and program which alone I came to believe, could win and preserve the national independence of Hindustan, my Motherland and enable her to render true service to humanity as well.

29. I have worked for several years in R.S.S. and subsequently joined the Hindu Mahasabha and volunteered myself to fight as a soldier under its pan-Hindu flag. About this time Veer Savarkar was elected to the Presidentship of the Hindu Mahasabha. The Hindu Sanghatan movement got verily electrified and vivified as never before, under his magnetic lead and whirl-wind propaganda. Millions of Hindu Sanghatanists looked up to him as the chosen hero, as the ablest and most faithful advocate of Hindu cause. I too was one of them. I worked devotedly to carry on the Mahasabha activities and hence came to be personally acquainted with Savarkarji.

30. Later on my friend and co-worker in the Hindu cause, Mr. Apte and myself decided to start a daily paper devoted to Hindu Sanghatan Movement. We met a number of prominent Hindu Sanghatanist leaders and after securing sympathy and financial help from them met Veer Savarkar as the President of the Mahasabha. He too sympathised with our project and advanced a sum of rupees fifteen thousand as his quota to the capital required, on condition that a limited company should be registered at our earliest convenience, and his advance should be transformed into number of shares.

31. Accordingly, we started the daily Marathi paper 'Daily Agrani' and after some period a limited company was registered. The sums advanced by Veer Savarkar and others were converted into shares of Rs. 500/- each. Amongst the directors and donors were such leading and respected gentlemen as Seth Gulab Chand (a brother of Shriman Seth Walchand Hirachandji), Mr. Shingre, an ex-Minrster of Bhor, Shreeman Bhalji Pendharkar — the film magnate of Kolhapur and others. Mr. Apte and myself were the Managing Directors of the Company. I was the editor solely responsible for the policy of the paper. We conducted the paper for years on strictly constitutional lines, and pleaded the policy of Hindu Sanghatan in general.

32. As press representatives of this daily, Mr. Apte and myself used to visit the Hindu Sanghatan office situated at Veer Savarkar's House in the middle hall of the ground floor of that house. This Hindu Sanghatan office was in the charge of Mr. G.V. Damle, the Secretary to Veer Savarkar. Mr. Appa Kasar was Veer Savarkar's body guard. We used to visit this office to secure from Mr. Damle, the Secretary, public statements issued by Veer Savarkar for the press in general; to note down other important information about the President's tours, interviews etc.

which his Secretary was authorised to publish. Mr. A.S. Bhide, who used to edit an English weekly namely 'Free Hindustan' was also residing with his family as a tenant in a set of rooms on the same ground-floor. The second reason why Mr. Apte and I used to visit Savarkar Sadan was to see Messrs Bhide, Damle, Kasar and other Hindu Sabha workers who used to gather at the Hindu Sanghatan office and had been personal friends to each other. Whenever we went to Bombay, we used to go to this office to meet all of them and have friendly chats. Sometimes we used to discuss the Hindu Sanghatan work with them. Some of them used to help us in securing advertisements for our paper.

33. But it must be specifically noted that these used to be our casual visits to Savarkar Sadan and were restricted generally to this Hindu Sanghatan Office, situated on the ground floor, for the above mentioned reasons. Veer Savarkar was residing on the first floor of the house. It was only very rarely that we could interview Veer Savarkar personally and that too by special appointment.

34. About three years ago, Veer Savarkar's health got seriously impaired and since then he was generally confined to bed. He thereafter suspended all his public activities and more or less had retired from public life. Thus deprived of his virile leadership and magnetic influence, the activities and influence of the Hindu Mahasabha too got crippled. And when Dr. Mookerjee became its President, the Mahasabha was actually reduced to the position of a hand-maid to the Congress. It became quite incapable of counteracting the dangerous anti-Hindu activities of Gandhite cabal on the one hand and the Muslim League on the other. Seeing this I lost all hope in the efficiency of the policy of running the Hindu Sanghatan movement on the constitutional lines of the Mahasabha

and began to shift for myself. I determined to organise a youthful band of Hindu Sanghatanists and adopt a fighting program both against the Congress and the League without consulting any of those prominent but old leaders of the Mahasabha.

35. I shall just mention here a few instances only, out of a number of them which painfully opened my eyes about this time to the fact that Veer Savarkar and other old leaders of Mahasabha could no longer be relied upon by me and the Hindu youths, to guide or even to appreciate the fighting program with which we aimed to counteract Gandhiji's activities from inside and the Muslim League from outside. In 1946 or thereabout the Muslim atrocities perpetrated on the Hindus under the Government patronage of Suhrawardy in Noakhali, made our blood boil. Our shame and indignation knew no bounds, when we saw that Gandhiji had come forward to shield that very Suhrawardy and began to style him as *'Shahid Saheb'*—a Martyr Soul (!) even in his prayer meetings. Not only that even after coming to Delhi, Gandhiji began to hold his prayer meetings in a Hindu temple in Bhangi Colony and persisted in reading passages from Quoran as a part of the prayer in that Hindu temple in spite of the protest of the Hindu worshippers there. Of course, he dared not read the Geeta in a mosque in the teeth of Muslim opposition. He knew what a terrible Muslim reaction would have been if he had done so. But he could safely trample over the feelings of the tolerant Hindus. To belie this belief, I determined to prove to Gandhiji that the Hindu too could be intolerant when his honour was insulted.

36. Mr. Apte and I decided to stage a series of demonstrations in Delhi during his meetings and make it impossible for him to hold such prayers. Mr. Apte with a large section of the refugees took out a procession in Delhi

condemning Gandhiji and his Shahid Suhrawardy and rushed into his prayer-meeting in the Bhangi Colony. Seeing the tumultuous protest that followed, Gandhiji slyly took shelter behind barred and guarded doors although at that time we had not the slightest idea of using any force.

37. But when Veer Savarkar read the report of this demonstration, instead of appreciating our move, he called me and blamed me privately for such anarchical tactics, even though this demonstration was peaceful. He said:

Just as I condemn the Congressites for breaking up your party meetings and election booths by disorderly conduct, I ought to condemn any such undemocratic conduct on the part of Hindu Sanghatanist also. If Gandhiji preached anti-Hindu teachings in his prayer meeting you should hold your party meetings and condemn his teachings. Amongst ourselves all different parties should conduct their propaganda on strictly constitutional lines.

38. The second leading incident took place just after this, when the partition of India was actually decided on. A group of Hindu Mahasabhaites wanted to know what the Hindu Mahasabha's attitude should be with regard to the Congress Government which was certain to be the Government of the New State, ruling over the so-called Indian State in the remaining part of India. Veer Savarkar and other top-ranking Hindu Mahasabha leaders quickly and emphatically said that any Indian Government formed to conduct such a freed Indian State should no longer be looked upon as a Government of a party—a Congress Government; but must be Honoured and obeyed as a National Government of Hindustan. Howsoever they deplored the creation of Pakistan. Their future motto was to be loyal and all-out support to the newly born Free

Indian State. Thus alone in their opinion, would it be possible to safeguard the newly won Freedom. Any attempt to undermine the Indian State would bring in a Civil War and enable the Muslims to realise their sinful and secret mission to turn whole of India into Pakistan.

39. Me and my friends however returned unconvinced. We felt in our heart of hearts that time had come when we should bid good-bye to Veer Savarkar's lead and cease to consult him in our future policy and program. Nor should we confide to him our future plans.

40. Just after that, followed the terrible outburst of Muslim fanaticism in Punjab and other parts of India. The Congress Government began to persecute, prosecute, and shoot the Hindus themselves who dared to resist the Muslim forces in Bihar, Calcutta, Punjab and other places. Our worst fears seemed to be coming true; and yet how painful and disgraceful it was for us to find that the 15th of August 1947 was celebrated with illumination and festivities, while the whole of the Punjab was set by the Muslims in flames and Hindu blood ran in rivers. The Hindu Mahasabhaites on my persuasion decided to boycott the festivities of the Congressite Government and to launch a fighting program to check the Muslim onslaughts.

41. The meeting of the Working Committee of the Hindu Mahasabha and the All-India Hindu Convention were held on or about 9th and 10th of August 1947, in Delhi, and Veer Savarkar presided. Mr. Apte and other friends and myself wanted to make a last effort to bring the Mahasabha and its veteran leaders like Veer Savarkar, Dr. Mookerjee, Mr. L.B. Bhopatkar and others to our views and to adopt a fighting resolution. The Mahasabha Working Committee did not accept our suggestion to appoint a council of action against Hyderabad or boycott

the Congress Government which was to run the newly created Stale of Divided India. To my mind to recognise a State of Divided India was tantamount to be a party to the cursed vivisection of India. The Working Committee passed a frothy resolution and asked the people to hoist the Bhagwa Flag on their houses on the day of August 15th, 1947. Veer Savarkar went further and actually insisted that the tri-colour flag with the wheel should be recognised as a National Flag. We openly resented his attitude.

42. Not only that on the 15th August, Veer Savarkar setting aside the will of the majority of Hindu Sanghatanists hoisted this new flag with the wheel, as a National Flag, on his house along with the Bhagwa. In addition to that when Dr. Mookerji asked his permission through a trunk call to Veer Savarkar as to whether Dr. Mookerji should accept a portfolio in the Indian Union Ministry. Veer Savarkar emphatically replied that the new Government must be recognised as a National Government and must be supported by all patriots and consequently Hindu Sanghatanists ought to extend their co-operation by accepting a portfolio if called upon to do so. He also congratulated the Congressite Ministers for the compromising attitude they were taking in calling on a Hindu Sabha leader like Dr. Mookerji to participate in the forming of National Ministry. Mr. Bhopatkar too supported Dr. Mookerji.

43. By this time it came to light that some top leaders of the Congress and some of their Provincial Ministers too had contacted Veer Savarkar and there was a brisk correspondence between them for forming a united front to support the new State, which policy Veer Savarkar had already advocated. I myself, could not be opposed to a common front of patriots, but while the Congress

Government continued to be sheepishly under the thumb of Gandhiji, while Gandhiji could thrust his anti-Hindu fads on the Congressite Government by restoring to such a simple trick as threatening a fast, it was clear to me that any common front under such circumstances was bound to be another form of setting up Gandhiji's Dictatorship and consequently a betrayal of Hindudom.

44. Every one of these steps taken by Veer Savarkar was so deeply resented by me that I, alongwith Mr. Apte and some of the young Hindu Sanghatanist friends decided once for all to chalk and work out our active program quite independently of the Mahasabha or its old veteran leaders. We resolved not to confide any of our new plans to any of them including Veer Savarkar.

45. I began to criticise the Hindu Maha Sabha and the policy of its old leaders in my daily paper 'Agrani' or 'Hindu Rashtra' and openly called upon the young generation of Hindu Sanghatanists to accept our own active program.

46. In order to work out my new independent program I decided to undertake two definite items in hand to begin with. The first item was to organise a series of powerful though peaceful demonstrations against Gandhiji so as to make him feel the impact of organised Hindu discontent, and to create confusion and disorder by demonstrative protests, etc. in his obnoxious prayer-meetings through which he carried out his anti-Hindu propaganda; and secondly to carry on an agitation against the Hyderabad State to defend our Hindu brothers and sisters near about the frontier line from the fanatic atrocities committed on them by the Muslims. As such a program could only be carried out on secret and dictatorial lines we resolved to divulge it only to those who believed in it and would obey our orders without questioning.

47. I would not have referred to the above details in this statement but for the learned prosecutor's opening speech in which he painted me as a mere tool in the hands of Veer Savarkar. This statement I felt to be a deliberate insult to my independence of judgment and action. The above facts had to be mentioned to dispel the incorrect impression about me, if any. Consequently, before I begin to narrate the rest of my statement, I re-assert that it is not true that Veer Savarkar had any knowledge of my activities which ultimately led me to fire shots at Gandhiji, I repeat that it is not true and it is totally false that either Mr. Apte in my presence or I myself told Badge that Veer Savarkar had given us an order to finish Gandhiji, Nehru and Suhrawardy as the approver is made to state falsely. It is not true that we ever took Badge to Veer Savarkar's house to take the last Darshan of Veer Savarkar in connection with any such plot or that Veer Savarkar ever said to us: *'Yashasvi houn ya'* [Be successful and come back]. Neither Mr. Apte in my presence nor I myself ever told Badge that Veer Savarkar told us that Gandhiji's hundred years were over and therefore we were bound to be successful. I was neither so superstitious as to crave for such blessings, nor so childish as to believe in such fortune-telling.

The news that Gandhi had decided to go on a fast to force India to transfer Rs 55 crores to Pakistan, was being broadcast over the news media in all languages. Pandit Nathuram Vinayak Godse and Narayan Dattatray Apte – the editor and manager of the 'Marathi Daily', the 'Hindu Rashtra', were sitting in their office and reading it on their teleprinter when they suddenly made their decision – 'Gandhi has to be killed'.

PART-II

GANDHIJI'S POLITICS X-RAYED

SECTION I

48. The back-ground to the event of 30th January, 1948 was wholly and exclusively political and I would like to explain it at some length. The fact that Gandhiji honoured the religious books of Hindus, Muslims and others or that he used to recite during his prayers verses from the Geeta, the Quoran and the Bible never provoked any ill will in me towards him. To my mind it is not at all objectionable to study comparative religion. Indeed it is a merit.

49. The territory bounded by the North Western Frontier in North and Cape Comorin in the South and the areas between Karachi and Assam that is the whole of pre-partition India has always been to me, my motherland. In this vast area, live people of various faiths and I hold that these creeds should have full and equal freedom for following their ideals and beliefs. In this area the Hindus are the most numerous of the lot. They have no place which they can call their own beyond or outside this country. Hindusthan is thus both the motherland and the holy land for the Hindus from times immemorial. The Hindus owe its fame and glory, its culture and art, knowledge of science and philosophy largely to this country. Next to the Hindus the Muslims are numerically predominant. They made systematic inroads into this country since the 10th century and gradually succeeded in establishing Muslim rule over the greater part of India.

50. Before the advent of the British both Hindus and Muslims as a result of centuries of experience had come to

realise that the Muslims could not remain as masters in India; nor could they be driven away here. Both had clearly understood that both had to stay here. Owing to the rise of the Maharattas, the revolt of the Rajputs and the uprise of the Sikhs, the Muslim hold on the country had become very feeble and although some of them continued to aspire for supremacy in India, practical people could see clearly that such hopes were futile. On the other hand the British had proved more powerful in battle and intrigue than either the Hindus or the Muslims. By their adoption of improved methods of administration and the assurance of the security to the life and property without any discrimination to both the Hindus and the Muslims, they accepted them as inevitable. Differences between Hindus and Muslims did exist even before the British came. Nevertheless it is a fact that the British made the most unscrupulous use of these differences and created more differences in order to maintain their power and authority. The Indian National Congress which was started with the object of winning power for the people in the governance of the country, had from the beginning kept before it the ideal of complete nationalism which implies that all Indians should enjoy equal rights and complete equality on the basis of democracy. This ideal of removing the foreign rule and replacing it by the democratic power and authority of the people appealed to me most from the very start of my public career.

51. In my writings and speeches I have always advocated that the religious and communal consideration should be entirely eschewed in the public affairs of the country; at elections, inside and outside the legislatures and in the making and unmaking of Cabinets. I have throughout stood for a secular State with joint electorates. To my mind this is the only sensible thing to do. (Here I

read extracts from the resolutions passed at the Bilaspur Session of Hindu Mahasabha held in December, 1944. Annexure Pages 12 and 13). Under the influence of the Congress this ideal was steadily making headway amongst the Hindus. But the Muslims as a community first stood aloof and later on under the corroding influence of the Divide and Rule Policy of the foreign masters were encouraged to cherish the ambition of dominating the Hindus. The first indication of this outlook was the demand for separate electorates instigated by the then Viceroy, Lord Minto in 1906. The British Government accepted this demand under the excuse of minority protection. While the Congress Party offered a verbal opposition, it progressively supported separatism by ultimately adopting the notorious formula of neither accepting nor rejecting in 1934.

52. Thus, originated and intensified, the demand for the disintegration of this country. What was the thin end of the wedge in the beginning became Pakistan in the end. The mistake however had begun with the laudable object of bringing out a united front amongst all classes in India in order to drive out the foreigners and it was hoped that separatism would eventually disappear.

53. In spite of my advocacy of joint electorates in principle I reconciled myself with the temporary introduction of separate electorates since the Muslims were keen on them. I however insisted that representation should be granted in strict proportion to the number of every community and no more. I have uniformly maintained this stand.

54. Under the inspiration of our British masters on the one hand and the encouragement by the Congress under Gandhiji's leadership on the other, the Muslim League

went on increasing its demands on communal basis. The Muslim community continuously backed the Muslim League. Each successive election proved that the Muslim League was able to bank on the fanaticism and ignorance of the Muslim masses and the League was thus encouraged, in its policy of separatism on an ever increasing scale year after year.

55. As I have stated before despite their objection to the principle of communal electorates, the unreasonable demands of the Muslim League were conceded by the Congress. Firstly by the Lucknow Pact of 1916 and at each successive revision of the constitution thereafter. This lapse, from nationalism and democracy on the part of the Congress, has proved an expensive calamity as the sequel has shown.

56. Since the year 1920, that is to say after the demise of Lokamanaya Tilak, Gandhiji's influence in the Congress first increased and then became supreme. His activities for public awakening were phenomenal in their intensity and were reinforced by the slogan of truth and non-violence which he ostentatiously paraded before the country. No sensible or enlightened person could object to these slogans. In fact there is nothing new or original in them. They are implicit in every constitutional public movement. To imagine that the bulk of mankind is or can ever become capable of scrupulous adherence to these lofty principles in its normal life from day to day is a mere dream. In fact, honour, duty and love of one's own kith and kin and country might often compel us to disregard non-violence and to use force. I could never conceive that an armed resistance to the aggressive is unjust. I will consider it is a religious and moral duty to resist, and if possible, to overpower such an enemy by the use of force. Shree Ramchandra killed

Ravan in a tumultuous fight and relieved Sita. Shree Krishna killed Kansa to end his wickedness. In the Mahabharat Arjun had to fight and slay, quite a number of his friends and relations including the revered Bhishma, because the latter was on the side of the aggressor. It is my firm belief that in dubbing Rama, Krishna and Arjuna as guilty of violence is to betray a total ignorance of the springs of human action. It was the heroic fight put up by the Chhatrapati Shivaji Maharaj that first checked and eventually destroyed Muslim tyranny in India. It was absolutely correct tactics for Shivaji to kill Afzul Khan as the latter would otherwise have surely killed him. In condemning Shivaji, Rana Pratap and Guru Govind as misguided patriots, Gandhiji has merely exposed his self-conceit.

57. Each of the heroes in his time resisted aggression on our country, protected the people against the atrocities and outrages by alien fanatics and won back the motherland from the invader. On the other hand during more than thirty years of the undisputed leadership of the Mahatma there were more desecration of temples, more forcible and fraudulent conversions, more outrages on women and finally the loss of one third of the country. It is therefore astounding that his followers cannot see what is clear even to the blind, viz. that the Mahatma was a mere pigmy before Shivaji, Rana Pratap and Guru Govind. His condemnation of these illustrious heroes was to say the least, most presumptuous.

58. The clique which has got into power with the patronage of British imperialism by a cowardly surrender to the Partition of India at the point of Muslim violence is now trying to exploit Gandhiji's death in hundred hectic ways for its own selfish aims. But history will give to them their proper place in the niche of fame. Gandhiji was,

paradoxical as it may appear, a violent pacifist who brought untold calamities on the country in the name of truth and non-violence, while Rana Pratap, Shivaji and the Guru will remain enshrined in the hearts of their countrymen for ever and for the freedom they brought to them.

59. As pointed out herein below Gandhiji's political activities can be conveniently divided under three heads. He returned to India from England some time about the end of 1914 and plunged into the public life of the country almost immediately. Unfortunately soon after his arrival Sir Pherozeshah Mehta and Mr. G.K. Gokhale, the latter whom Gandhiji called his Guru, died within a short span of time. Gandhiji began his work by starting an Ashram in Ahmedabad on the banks of the Sabarmati river, and made Truth and nonviolence his slogans. He himself has admitted that he had often acted contrary to his professed principles and if it was for appeasing the Muslims, he hardly had any scruple in doing so. Truth and non-violence are most excellent as an ideal and admirable as guides in action. They are, however, to be practised in actual day-to-day life and not in the air. I am showing later on that Gandhiji himself was guilty of glaring breaches of his much vaunted ideals.

60. Gandhiji's political career will be divided as already stated under three heads:

(i) The period between 1915 to 1939-40.

(ii) The period between 1939-40 to 3rd June, 1947, when the Indian National Congress surrendered to Mr. Jinnah and accepted Pakistan under the leadership of the Mahatma.

(iii) The period between the date of partition to the day of his last fast unto death resulting in the payment of Rs. 55 crores to Pakistan and the Mahatama's death within a short period.

61. When Gandhiji finally returned to India at the end of 1914, he brought with him a very high, reputation for courageous leadership of Indians in South Africa. He had placed himself at the head of the struggle for the assertion and vindication of the national self-respect of India and for our rights of citizenship against white tyranny in that country. He was honoured and obeyed by Hindus, Muslims and Parsees alike and was universally acclaimed as the leader of all Indians in South Africa. His simplicity of life, his unselfish devotion to the cause which he had made his own, his self-sacrifice and earnestness in fighting against the racial arrogance of the Africanders had raised the prestige of Indians. In India he had endeared himself to all.

62. When he returned here to serve his countrymen in their struggle for freedom, he had legitimately hoped that as in Africa he would command the unchallenged confidence and respect of all communities. But in this hope he soon found himself disappointed. India was not South Africa. In South Africa, Indians had claimed nothing but elementary rights of citizenship which were denied to them. They had all a common and acute grievance. The Boer and the British both had treated them like door mats. Hindus, Muslims and Parsees therefore stood united like one man against the common enemy. They had no other quarrel with the South African Government. The Indian problem at home was quite different. We were fighting for home rule, self-government and even for Independence. We were intent on overthrowing an Imperial Power, which was firmly entrenched in the soil. It was determined to continue its sway over us, by all possible means including the policy of 'Divide and Rule' which had intensified the cleavage between the Hindus and Muslims. Gandhiji was thus confronted at the very outset with a problem, the like of which he had never experienced in South Africa. In South

Africa he had smooth sailing throughout. The identity of interest between the various communities there was complete and every Indian had ranged himself behind him. But in India communal franchise, separate electorates and the like had already undermined the solidarity of the nation, more of such happenings were in the offing and the sinister policy of communal favouritism was being pursued by the British with the utmost tenacity without any scruple. Gandhiji therefore, found it most difficult to obtain the unquestioned leadership of the Hindus and the Muslims in India as in South Africa. But he had been accustomed to be the leader of all Indians and quite frankly, he could not understand the leadership of a divided country. It was absurd for his honest mind to think of accepting the generalship of an army divided against itself.

63. For the first five years after his return to India there was not much scope for the attainment of supreme leadership in Indian politics by him. Dadabhai Naoroji, Sir Pherozeshah Mehta, Lokmanya Tilak and Mr. G.K. Gokhale and others were still alive and Gandhiji though honoured, and popular was, still a junior compared to those veterans both in age and experience. But an inexorable fate removed all of them in five years and with the death of Lokmanya Tilak in August, 1920 Gandhiji was at once thrown into the front line.

64. He saw that the foreign rulers by the policy of 'Divide and Rule' were corrupting the patriotism of the Muslims and there was little chance of his leading a united host to the battle for Freedom unless he was able to inculcate the feeling and common devotion to the Motherland in them. He, therefore, made Hindu-Muslim unity the foundation of his politics. As a counterblast to the British tactics he started making the most friendly approaches to the Muslim community and reinforced them

by making generous and extravagant promises to the Muslims. This, of course, was not wrong in itself so long as it was done consistently with India's struggle for democratic national freedom. But Gandhiji completely forgot this, the most essential aspect of his campaign for unity, with the consequencies we all know by now.

65. Our British rulers were able, to make concessions to Muslims continuously and the various communities divided. By 1919 Gandhiji had become desperate in his endeavours to get the Muslims to trust him and went from one absurd promise to another. He promised 'a blank cheque' to the Muslims. He backed the Khilafat movement in 'this country and was able to enlist the full support of the National Congress in that policy. For a time, Gandhiji appeared to succeed and the prominent Muslim leaders in India became his followers. Mr. Jinnah was nowhere in 1920-21, and the Ali Brothers became de-facto Muslim leaders. Gandhiji welcomed this situation as he foresaw the promise of leadership of the Muslims. He made most of the Ali Brothers, raised them to the skies by flattery and unending concessions; but what he wanted, never happened. The Muslims ran the Khilafat Committee as a distinct political religious organisation and throughout maintained it as a separate entity from the Congress; and very soon the Moplah Rebellion showed that the Muslims had not the slightest idea of national unity on which Gandhiji had set his heart and had staked so much. There followed, as usual in such cases, a huge slaughter of the Hindus, numerous forcible conversions; rape and arson. The British Government entirely unmoved by the rebellion suppressed it in a few months and left to Gandhiji the joy of his Hindu-Muslim unity. The Khilafat agitation had failed and let down Gandhiji. British Imperialism emerged stronger, the Muslims became more fanatical and the

consequences were borne by the Hindus. But undaunted by the tactics of the British rulers, Gandhiji became more stubborn in the pursuit of his phantom task of Hindu-Muslim unity. By the Act of 1919 separate electorates were enlarged and communal representation was continued not merely in the legislature and the local bodies but was even extended within the Cabinet. The jobs began to be distributed on communal basis and the Muslims obtained high jobs from our British Masters not on merit but by remaining aloof from the struggle for freedom and because of their being the followers of Islam. Government patronage to Muslims in the name of minority protection penetrated throughout the body-politic of the Indian State and the Mahatama's meaningless slogans were no match against this wholesale corruption of the Muslim mind. But Gandhiji did not relent. He still lived in the hope of becoming the common leader both of the Hindus and the Muslims. The more he got defeated, the more, he indulged in encouraging the Muslims by extravagant-methods. The position continued to deteriorate and by 1925 it became clear to all, that the Government had won all along the line. Like the proverbial gambler Gandhiji increased his stake. He agreed to the separation of Sind and the creation of a separate province in the North-West Frontier. He also went on conceding to one undemocratic demand after another to the Muslim League in the vain hope of enlisting its support in the national struggle. By this time the stock of the Ali Brothers had gone down and Mr. Jinnah who had staged a come-back was having the best of both the worlds. Whatever concessions the Government and the Congress made, Mr. Jinnah accepted and asked for more. Separation of Sind from Bombay and the creation of the North-West Frontier province, were followed by the Round Table Conference in which the minority question loomed large. Mr. Jinnah stood out against the federation until Gandhiji himself requested Mr. McDonald, the Labour Premier, to give the Communal Award. Further seeds were thereby sown for the disintegration of this country. The communal principle became deeply imbedded in the Reforms of 1935. Mr. Jinnah took the fullest advantage of every situation. The Federation of India which was to consolidate Indian Nationhood was in fact, defeated. Mr. Jinnah had never taken kindly to it. The Congress continued to support the Communal Award under the very hypocritical words of neither supporting nor opposing, which really meant its tactic acceptance. During the War, 1939-44, Mr. Jinnah took up openly one stand,—a sort of benevolent neutrality—and promised to support the war as soon as the Muslim rights were conceded. In April 1940, within six months of the War, Mr. Jinnah came out with the demand for Pakistan on the basis of his two nation theory. Mr. Jinnah totally ignored the fact that there were Hindus and Muslims in large numbers in every part of India. There may be a majority of Hindus in some case and Muslims in other Provinces and vice versa. There was no Province in India where either the Hindus or the Muslims were negligible in numbers. Any division of India would leave the minority question wholly unsolved.

66. The British Government liked the Pakistan idea as it kept the Hindus and Muslims estranged during the war and thereby avoided embarrassing the Government. The Muslims did not obstruct the war efforts and the Congress sometimes remained neutral and some times opposed to it. On the other hand the Hindu Sabha realised that this was an opportunity for our young men to have a military training, which is absolutely essential for our nation, from which we were rather kept far away intentionally by the British. Due to this war, the doors of

Army, Navy and Air-force were opened to us, and Mahasabha urged our countrymen to militarise Hindus. The result was that nearly half a million Hindus learnt the art of warfare and mastered the mechanised aspect of modern warfare. The Congress Governments are enjoying the fruits of the Mahasabha's foresight because the troops they are using in Kashmir and Hyderabad would not have been there ready but for the effort of men with such outlook. The Congress-in 1942, started the 'Quit India' movement in the name of Freedom. Violent outrages were perpetrated by Congress men in every Province. In the Province of North Bihar there was hardly a railway station which was not burnt or destroyed by the Congress non-cooperators. In spite of all the opposition of the Congress. The Germans were beaten in April, 1945 and the Japanese in August, 1945. The atomic bomb brought the collapse of the Japanese resistance and the British won against Japanese and Germans. In spite of the opposition of the Congress party, the 'Quit India campaign of 1942 had completely failed. Britishers had triumphed and the Congress leaders decided to come to terms with them. Indeed in the subsequent years the Congress policy can be quite correctly described as *'Peace at any Price'* and *'Congress in Office at all costs'*. The Congress compromised with the British who placed it in office and in return the Congress surrendered to the violence of Mr. Jinnah; carved out one-third of India to him, an explicitly racial and theological State and destroyed two million human beings in the process. Pandit Nehru now professes again and again that the Congress stands for a secular State and violently denounces those who reminded him that only last year he agreed to a communal and theological State. His vociferous adherence to a 'Secular State' is nothing but a case of *'my lady protests too much.'*

67. The 'Quit India' movement had to be abandoned. The Congress support to the war against Japan had to be assured and the Viceroy Lord Wavell had to be accepted as the head of the Government of India, before the Congress was to be called into the Conference Chamber.

68. This section summarises the background of the agony of India's partition and the tragedy of Gandhiji's assassination. Neither the one nor the other gives me any pleasure to record or to remember, but the Indian people and the world at large ought to know the history of the last thirty years during which India has been torn into pieces by the Imperialist policy of the British and under a mistaken policy of communal unity. The Mahatma was betrayed into action which has ultimately led not to the Hindu-Muslim unity, but to the shattering of the whole basis of that unity. Five crores Indian Muslims have ceased to be our countrymen; virtually the non-Muslim minority in Western Pakistan have been liquidated either by the most brutal murders or by a forced tragic removal from their moorings of centuries; the same process is furiously at work in Eastern Pakistan. One Hundred and ten millions of people have become torn from their homes of which not less than four millions are Muslims. When I found that even after such terrible results, Gandhiji continued to pursue the same policy of appeasement, my blood boiled, and I could not tolerate him any longer. I do not mean to use hard words against Gandhiji personally nor do I wish to conceal my utter dissent from the disapproval of the very foundation of his policy and methods. Gandhiji in fact succeeded in doing what the British always wanted to do in pursuance of their policy of 'Divide and Rule', He helped them in dividing India and it is not yet certain whether their rule has ceased.

Gandhiji's Politics X-rayed

SECTION II

69. The accumulating provocation of 32 years, culminating in his last pro-Muslim fast at last goaded me to the conclusion, that the existence of Gandhiji should be brought to an end immediately. On coming back to India he developed a subjective mentality under which he alone was to be the final judge of what was right or wrong. If the country wanted his leadership it had to accept his infallibility, if it did not, he would stand aloof from the Congress and carry on in his own way. Against such an attitude there can be no half way house; either the Congress had to surrender its will to his and had to be content with playing the second fiddle to all his eccentricity, whimsicality, metaphysics and primitive vision, or it had to carry on without him. He alone was the judge of every one and everything; he was the master brain guiding the civil disobedience movement; nobody else knew the technique of that movement; he alone knew when to begin it and when to withdraw it. The movement may succeed or fail; it may bring untold disasters and political reverses but that could make no difference to the Mahatma's infallibility. 'A Satyagrahi can never fail' was his formula for declaring his own infallibility and nobody except himself knew who a Satyagrahi was. Thus Gandhiji became the judge and the counsel in his own case. These childish inanities and obstinacies coupled with a most severe austerity of life, ceaseless work and lofty character made Gandhiji formidable and irresistible. Many people thought his politics were irrational but they had either to withdraw from the Congress or to place their intelligence at his feet to do what he liked with it. In a position of such absolute irresponsibility, Gandhiji was guilty of blunder after blunder, failure after failure, and disaster after disaster.

No one single political victory can be claimed to his credit during 33 years of his political predominance. Herein I mention below in some detail the series of blunders which he committed during 32 years of his undisputed leadership.

70. I shall now describe briefly the enormous mischief done by the slogans and the nostrums which Gandhiji prescribed and followed, in pursuance of his policy, the fatal results that we now know. Here are some of them:

(a) ***Khilafat***—As a result of the First World War, Turkey had lost most of its Empire in Africa and the Middle East. It had lost all its European Imperial possessions. By 1914 only a strip of land was all that was left to her on the continent of Europe. The young Turks had forced the Sultan of Turkey to abdicate and with the disappearance of the Sultan the Khilafat was also abolished. The Indian Muslims' devotion to the Khilafat was strong and earnest and they believed that it was Britain that had brought about the downfall of the Sultan and the Khilafat. They therefore started a campaign for the revival of the Khilafat. In the moment of opportunism, the Mahatma misconceived the idea that by helping the Khilafat Movement he would become the leader of the Muslims in India as he already was of the Hindus. With the Hindu-Muslim unity thus achieved, the British would soon have to concede Swaraj. But again, Gandhiji miscalculated and by leading the Indian National Congress to identify itself with the Khilafat Movement. He quite gratuitously introduced religions elements which has proved a tragic and expensive calamity. For the moment the movement for the revival of the Khilafat appeared to be succeeding. The Muslims who were not with the Khilafat Movement soon became out of date and the Ali Brothers who were its foremen, swam on the wave of popularity and carried everything whatever was before them. Mr. Jinnah found himself a lonely figure and was of no significance for a few years. The movement however failed. Our British Masters were not unduly shaken and as a combined result of repression and the Montague Chelmsford Reforms they were able to tide over the Khilafat Movement in a few years time. The Muslims had kept the Khilafat Movement distinct from the Congress all along. They welcomed the Congress support but they did not merge with it. When failure came, the Muslims became desperate with disappointment and their anger was borne by the Hindus. Innumerable riots in the various parts of India followed. The chief victims were the Hindus everywhere. The Hindu-Muslim unity of the Mahatma became a mirage.

(b) **Moplah Rebellion**—Malabar, Punjab, Bengal and N.W.F. Province were the scenes of repeated outrages on the Hindus. The Moplah rebellion as it was called was the most prolonged and concentrated attack on the Hindu religion, Hindu honour, Hindu life and Hindu property; hundreds of Hindus were forcibly converted to Islam, women were outraged. The Mahatma who had brought about all this calamity on India by his communal policy kept mum. He never uttered a single word of reproach against the aggressors nor did he allow the Congress to take any active steps whereby repetition of such outrages could be prevented. On the other hand he went to the length of denying the numerous cases of forcible conversions in Malabar and actually published in his paper 'Young India' that there was only one case of forcible conversion. His own Muslim friends informed him that he was wrong and that the forcible conversions were numerous in Malabar. He never corrected his misstatements but went to the absurd length of starting a relief fund for the Moplahs instead of their victims. The promised land of Hindu-Muslim unity was not yet in sight.

(c) **Afghan Amir Intrigue**—When the Khilafat movement failed, Ali Brothers decided to do something which might keep alive the Khilafat sentiments. Their slogan was that whoever was the enemy of the Khilafat was also the enemy of Islam. As the British were chiefly responsible for the defeat and the dethronement of the Sultan of Turkey, every faithful Muslim was in solemn duty bound to be a bitter enemy of Britain. With that object they secretly intrigued to invite the Amir of Afghanistan to invade India and promised him every support, there is a long history behind this intrigue. Ali brothers never denied their share in the conspiracy. The Mahatma pursued his tactics of getting Hindu-Muslim unity by supporting the Ali brothers through thick and through thin. He publicly poured his affection on them and promised them unstinted support in the restoration of the Khilafat. Even with regard to the invasion of India by the Amir, the Mahatma directly and indirectly supported the Ali Brothers. This is proved beyond the shadow of a doubt. The late Mr. Shastri, Mr. C.Y. Chintamani the Editor of the 'Leader' of Allahabad and even the Mahatma's lifelong friend, the Late Rev. C.F. Andrews told him quite clearly that his speeches and writings amounted to a definite support to the Ali Brothers in their invitation to the Amir of Afghanistan to invade India. The following quotation from the Mahatma's writing in those days should make it clear that he had forgotten his own country in his one consuming desire to please the Muslims had become a party to the invasion of his motherland by a foreign Ruler. The Mahatma supported the invasion in the following words:

I cannot understand why the Ali Brothers are going to be arrested as the rumors go, and why I am to remain free. They have done nothing which I would not do. If they had sent a message to Amir, I also would send one to inform the Amir that if he came, no Indian so long as I can help it, would help the Government to drive him back.

The vigilance of the British broke the conspiracy. Nothing came out of the Ali Brothers' grotesque scheme to the invasion of India and Hindu-Muslim unity remained as far away as before.

(d) (i) **Attack on Arya Samaj**—Gandhiji ostentatiously displayed his love for Muslim—by a most unworthy and unprovoked attack on the Arya Samaj in 1924.

He publicly denounced the Samaj for its supposed sins of omission and commission. It was an utterly unwarranted reckless and discreditable attack, but whatever would please the Mohammedans was the heart's desire of Gandhiji. The Arya Samaj made a powerful but polite statement and for some time Gandhiji remained silent. The growing political influence of Gandhiji weakened the Arya Samaj. No follower of Swami Dayanand could possibly be a Gandhian Congressman in politics. The two things are entirely incompatible; but the lure of office and leadership has induced numerous Arya Samajists to play the double game of claiming to be Gandhite Congressmen and Arya Samajists at the same time. The result was that a ban on Satyartha Prakash was imposed by the Government of Sind four years ago. The Arya Samaj on the whole took it lying down. As a result its hold on Hindu social and religious life has been further considerably crippled. Individual members of the Samaj are and were strong nationalists. The late Lala Lajpat Rai, and Swami Shradhanand to mention only two names were staunch Arya Samajists but they were foremost amongst the leaders of the Congress till the end of their life. They did not stand for blind support to Gandhiji, but were definitely opposed to his pro-Muslim policy, and openly fought him on that issue. But these great men are gone now. We know that the bulk of the Arya Samaj continues to be what they always were, but they are ill-informed and badly led by the self-seeking section of the Samaj. The Samaj has ceased to be the force and the power that it was at one time.

(d)(ii) Gandhiji's attack did not improve his popularity with the Muslims but it provoked a Muslim youth to murder Swami Shradhanandji within a few months. The charge against the Samaj that it was a reactionary body was manifestly false. Everybody knew that far from being a reactionary body the Samaj had been the vanguard of social reforms among the Hindus.

The Samaj had for a hundred years stood for the abolition of untouchability long before the birth of Gandhiji. The Samaj had popularised widow re-marriage. The Samaj had denounced the caste system and preached the oneness of not merely the Hindus but of all those who were prepared to follow its tenets. Gandhiji was completely silence for some time. His leadership made the people forget his baseless attack on the Arya Samaj and even weakened the Samaj to a large extent. Swami Dayanand Saraswati who was the founder of the Arya Samaj had no fad about violence or non-violence. In his teaching the use of force was not ruled out but was permissible if morally desirable. It must have been a struggle for the leaders of the Arya Samaj whether to remain within the Congress or not. Gandhiji insisted on non-violence in all cases and Swami Dayanand made no bones about it. But Swamiji was dead and Gandhiji.'s star was ascendant in the political firmament.

(e) **Separation of Sind**—By 1928 Mr. Jinnah's stock had risen very high and the Mahatma had already conceded many unfair and improper demands of Mr. Jinnah at the expense of Indian democracy and the Indian Nation and the Hindus. The Mahatma even supported the separation of Sind from the Bombay presidency and threw the Hindus of Sind to the communal wolves. Numerous riots took place in Sind—Karachi, Sukkur, Shikarpur and where other places the Hindus were the only sufferers. The Hindu-Muslim unity receded further from the horizon.

(f) **League's Good Bye to Congress**—With each defeat Gandhiji became more keen on his method of achieving Hindu-Muslim unity. Like the gambler who had lost heavily, he became more desperate; increasing his stakes each time. He indulged in the most irrational concessions if only they could placate. Mr. Jinnah and enlist his support under the Mahatma's leadership in the fight for freedom. The aloofness of the Muslims from the Congress increased in the coming years. The Muslim League refused to have anything to do with the Congress after 1928. The resolution of Independence passed by the Congress at its Lahore Session in 1929 found the Muslims conspicuous by their absence and strongly aloof from the Congress organisation. The hope of Hindu Muslim unity was hardly entertained by anybody thereafter; but Gandhiji continued to be resolutely optimistic and surrendered more and more to Muslim communalism.

(g) **Round-Table Conference and Communal Award**—The British authorities both in India and in England, had realised that the demand for a bigger and truer instalment of constitutional reforms was most insistent and claimant in India. In spite of their unscrupulous policy of 'Divide and Rule' and the communal discord which it had generated. The resulting situation had brought them no permanence and security in India. They therefore decided by the end of 1929 to convene a Round Table Conference in England early in the next year and made a declaration to that effect. Mr. Ramsay McDonald was the Prime Minister and the Labour Government was in power. But the action was too late. The resolution of Independence was passed a month later at the Lahore Session of the Congress in spite of the aforesaid declaration and the Congress Party decided to boycott this Round Table Conference. Instead, a Salt Campaign was started after a few months which created tremendous enthusiasm and nearly 70,000 people went to jails in breaking the provisions of the Salt Act. The Congress however soon regretted its boycott of the First Round Table Conference and at the Karachi Congress of 1931 it was decided to send Gandhiji alone as the Congress Representative to Second Session of Round Table Conference. Anybody who reads the proceedings, of that Session will realise that Gandhiji was the biggest factor in bringing about the total failure of the Conference. Not even one of the decisions of the Round Table Conference was in support of democracy or nationalism. The Mahatma went to the length of inviting Mr. Ramsay Mc. Donald to give what was called the Communal Award, thereby strengthening the disintegrating forces of communalism which had already corroded the body politic for the past 24 years. The Mahatma was thus responsible for a direct and substantial intrusion of communal electorate and communal franchise in the future Parliament of India. There is no wonder that when the communal award was given by Mr. Ramsay McDonald, the Mahatma refused to oppose it and the members of the Assembly were asked 'Neither to support nor to reject it.' Gandhiji himself put an axe on the communal unity on which he had staked so much for the previous fifteen years. No wonder under the garb of minority protection we got in the Government of India Act of 1935, a permanent statutory recognition of communal franchise, communal electorate and even weightage for the minorities, especially the Muslims, both in the Provinces and in the Centre. Those elected on the communal franchise, would be naturally communal minded and would have no interest in bridging the gulf between communalism and nationalism. The formation of a parliamentary party on political and economic grounds thus became impossible. Hindus and Muslims became divided in opposite camps and worked as rival parties, placing increased momentum to separatism. Almost everywhere Hindus became victims of communal orgies at the hands of the Muslims. People became perfectly cynical about any possibility of unity between Hindus and Muslims but the Gandhiji kept on repeating his barren formula all the time. (Reference: Pandit Madan Mohan Malaviya's speech against the acceptance of Communal Award).

(h) **Acceptance of Offices and Resigning in Huff - Provincial Autonomy** was introduced from the 1st of April, 1937 under the Government of India Act 1935. The Act was bristling with safeguards. Special powers, protection to vested interests to the British and continuation of the existing British personnels in the various services were kept in tact. The Congress therefore would not accept office at first but soon found out that in every Province, a Ministry was constituted and that at least in five Provinces they were functioning in the normal manner. In the other six Provinces, the Ministers were in a minority but they were forging ahead with their nation building programme. The Congress felt that it would be left out in the cold if it persisted in its policy of barren negation. It therefore decided to accept office in July, 1937; in doing so it committed a serious blunder in excluding the members of the Muslim League from effective participation in the Cabinet. They only admitted into the Cabinet such Muslims as were congressmen. This was the right policy for a country with citizen franchise and without communal representation. But having accepted communal electorate and communal franchise and other paraphernalia of separatism, it became untenable to keep out the members of the Muslim League who represented the bulk of the Muslims in every province, where they were in a minority. The Nationalist Muslims who became Ministers were not representatives of the Muslims in the sense in which the Muslim League Members were and in not taking the League Members in the Cabinet the Congress openly repudiated its own action in statutorily having recognised itself communalist by statute. On the other hand the Muslims were quite unwilling to come under the Congress control. Their interest never needed protection. The Governors were there always ready and willing to offer the most sympathetic support. The rejection of Muslim League Members as Ministers gave Mr. Jinnah a tactical advantage which he utilised to the full. In 1939 when the Congress resigned Office in a huff, it completely played in the hands of the Muslim League and British Imperialism. Under Section 93 of the Government of India Act 1935 the Governments of the Congress Provinces were taken over by the Governors and the Muslim League Ministries remained in power and authority in the remaining Provinces. The Governors carried on the administration with a definite leaning towards the Muslims as an Imperial Policy of British. Communalism reigned right throughout the country through the Muslim Ministries on the one hand and the pro-Muslim Governors on the other. The Hindu-Muslim unity of Gandhiji became a dream, if it were ever anything else; but Gandhiji never cared. His ambition was to become the leader of Hindus and Muslims alike and in resigning from the Ministries the Congress again sacrificed democracy and nationalism. The fundamental rights of the Hindus, religious, political, economic and social, all were sacrificed at the altar of the Mahatmic obstinacy.

(i) **League Taking Advantage of War**—Encouraged by the situation thus created, the Muslim Government in five Provinces and the pro-Muslim Governors in the other six, Mr. Jinnah went ahead in full speed. The Congress opposed the war in one way or another. Mr. Jinnah and the League had a very clear policy. They remained neutral and created no trouble for the Government; but in the following year, at the Lahore session of the Muslim League passed a resolution for the partition of India as a condition for their co-operation in the war. Lord Linlithgow within a few months of the Lahore Resolution gave full support to the Muslims in their policy of separation by a declaration of Government Policy which assured the Muslims that no change in the political constitution of India will be made without the consent of all the elements in India's national life. The Muslim League and Mr. Jinnah were thus vested with a veto over the political progress of this country by the pledge given by the Viceroy of India. From that day the process of disintegration advanced with accumulated force. Muslims were not prohibited by the League from getting recruited to the Army, Navy and Air Force and they did so in large numbers. In fact the Punjab Muslims resented their percentage in the Indian Army at all reduced. Thus with a view to preparing for eventualities in a future Muslim State as is being done in Kashmir today, and of course the Muslim League never created any difficulty for the Government throughout the six years of the global war (Refer to the speech of late Sir Sikandar Hyat Khan delivered at Cairo before armed forced during the last World War). All that they wanted was that no changes should be made in the Constitution of India without their full consent, and that full consent, could be obtained if only Pakistan was conceded. This assurance was virtually given by Lord Linlithgow in August, 1940.

(j) **Cripp's Partition Proposal Accepted**—The Congress did not know its own mind as to whether it should support the war, oppose or remain neutral. All these attitudes were expressed in turn one after the other; sometimes by way of speeches, sometimes by way of resolutions, sometimes through Press campaigns and sometimes in other ways. Government naturally felt that the Congress has no mind of its own except verbose condemnation. The war was carried on without let or hindrance till 1942. The Government could get all the men, all the money, and all the material which their war efforts needed. Every Government loan was fully subscribed. In 1942 came the Cripps Mission. It presented to the Congress and to the rest of India, Dead Sea Apple of useless promises, coupled with a clear hint of partition of India in the background. Naturally the Mission failed, but the Congress while opposing the Mission's proposal yielded to the principle of partition after a very pretentious resolution reiterating its adherence to democracy and nationalism. At a meeting of the All India Congress Committee held in April, 1942 at Allahabad the principle of partition was repudiated by an overwhelming majority—the minority consisting of the present Governor General Mr. C. Rajagopalchari and his half a dozen supporters.—But Maulana Azad, the so called nationalist Muslim, was then the President of the Congress. A few months later he gave a ruling that the Allahabad Resolution had no effect on the earlier resolution of the Working Committee which conceded the principle of Pakistan however remotely. The Congress was entirely at the end of its wits. The British Government went on effectively controlling the whole country through Muslim Ministries and through pro-Muslim Governors. The Princes wholly identified themselves with the war. Labour refused to keep aloof. The capitalist class supported the Congress in words and in deed by supplying the Government everything it wanted at top prices. Even Khaddar enthusiasts sold blankets to Government. The Congress could see no way out of its absolute paralysis; it was out of office and Government carried on in spite of its nominal opposition.

(k) **'Quit India' by Congress and 'Divide and Quit' by League**—Out of sheer desperation Gandhiji evolved the 'Quit India' Policy which was endorsed by the Congress. It was supposed to be the greatest national rebellion against foreign rule. Gandhiji had ordered the people to 'do or die'. Except that the leaders were quickly arrested and detained behind the prison bars some furtive acts of violence were practised by congressmen for some weeks, but in less than three months the whole movement was throttled by the Government; in firmness and discretion. The movement soon collapsed. What remained, was a series of piteous appeals by the Congress Press and the Congress supporters, who were outside the jail, for the release of the arrested leaders without formally withdrawing the 'Quit India' movement, which had already collapsed. Gandhiji even staged a fast for his release, but for two years until the Germans were decisively beaten, the leaders had to remain in jails and our Imperial masters were triumphant all along. Mr. Jinnah openly opposed the 'Quit India' Movement as hostile to the Muslims and raised a counter slogan 'Divide and Quit'. That is where Gandhiji's Hindu-Muslim unity had arrived.

(l) **Hindi versus Hindustani**—Absurdly pro-Muslim policy of Gandhiji is nowhere more blatantly illustrated than in his perverse attitude on the question of the National Language of India. By all the tests of a scientific language, Hindi has the most prior claim to be accepted as the National Language of this country. In the beginning of his career in India, Gandhiji gave a great impetus to Hindi but as he found that the Muslims did not like it, he became a turncoat and blossomed forth as the champion of what is called Hindustani. Every body in India knows that there is no language called Hindustani; it has no grammar, it has no vocabulary; it is a mere dialect; it is spoken but not written. It is a bastard tongue and a crossbreed between Hindi and Urdu and not even the Mahatma's sophistry could make it popular. In his desire to please the Muslims he insisted that Hindustani alone should be the national language of India. His blind supporters of course blindly supported him and the so-called hybrid tongue began to be used. Words like *'Badshah Ram'* and *'Begum Sita'* were spoken and written, but the Mahatma never dared to speak of Mr. Jinnah as Shri Jinnah and Maul ana Azad as Pandit Azad. All his experiments were at the expense of the Hindus. His was a one-way traffic in his search of Hindu-Muslim unity. The charm and the purity of the Hindi language was to be prostituted to please the Muslims. Even Congressmen, from the rest of India, refused to digest this nostrum. He continued to persist in his support to Hindustani. The bulk of the Hindus however proved to be stronger and more loyal to their culture and to their mother tongue and refused to bow down to the Mahatmic fiat. The result was that Gandhiji did not prevail in the Hindi Parishad and had to resign from that body. His pernicious influence however remains and the Congress Governments in India still hesitate whether to select Hindi or Hindustani as the National language of India. The barest common sense should make it clear to the meanest intelligence that the language of 80 per cent of the people must be the language of the country but his ostentatious support of the Muslims made him look almost idiotic when he continued to stand for Hindustani. Happily there are millions and millions of champions of the Hindi language and the Devnagari script. The U.P. Government has adopted Hindi as the language of the Province. The Committee appointed by the Government of India has translated the whole of the Draft Constitution in pure Hindi. It now remains for the Congress Party in the legislature to adopt the commonsense view in favour of Hindi or assert their loyalty to the Mahatma in their mad endeavour to force a language on a great country like India. For practical purpose Hindustani is only Urdu under a different name, but Gandhiji could not have the courage to advocate the adoption of Urdu as against Hindi, hence the subterfuge to smuggle Urdu under the garb of Hindustani. Urdu is not banned by any nationalist Hindu but to smuggle it under the garb of Hindustani is a fraud and a crime, that is what the Mahatma tried to do. To bolster up a dialect in School Curriculum and in educational institutions that non-existent language in the garb of Hindustani because it pleased the Muslims was the communalism of the worst type on the part of the Mahatma. All these for Hindu-Muslim unity.

(m) **Vande Mataram Not to be Sung**—The infatuation of Gandhiji for the Muslims and his incorrigible craving for Muslim leadership without any regard for right or wrong, for truth or justice, and in utter contempt of the sentiments of the Hindus as a whole was the high watermark of the Mahatmic benevolence. It is notorious that some Muslims disliked the celebrated song of 'Vande Mataram' and the Mahatma forthwith stopped its singing or recital wherever he could. This song has been honoured for a century as the most inspiring exhortation to the Bengalees to stand up, like one mass for their nation. In the anti-partition agitation of 1905, in Bengal the song came to a special prominence and popularity. The Bengalees swore by it and dedicated themselves to the Motherland at countless meetings where this song was sung. The British Administrator did not understand the true meaning of the song which simply meant 'Hail Motherland.' Government therefore banned its singing forty years ago for some time. That led to its increased popularity all over the country. It continued to be sung at all Congress and other national gatherings but as soon as one Muslim objected to it, Gandhiji utterly disregarded the national sentiment behind it and persuaded the Congress, not to insist upon the singing as the national song. We are now asked to adopt Rabindranath Tagore's 'Jana Gana Mana', as a substitute for 'Vande Mataram'. Could anything be more demoralising or pitiful than this brazen-faced action against a song of world-wide fame? Simply because one ignorant fanatic disliked it. The right way to proceed would have been to enlighten the ignorant and remove the prejudice. But that is the policy which during the thirty years of unbounded popularity and leadership Gandhiji could not muster courage to try. His Hindu-Muslim unity idea only meant to surrender, capitulate, and concede whatever the Muslims wanted. No wonder, the 'Will O' the Wasp' unity never came and never could have come.

(n) **Shiva Bavani Banned**—Gandhiji banned the public recital or perusal of Shiva Bavani a beautiful collection of 52 verses by a Hindu poet in which he had extoled the great power of Shivaji and the protection which he brought to the Hindu community and the Hindu religion. The refrain of that collection says, "*If there were no Shivaji, the entire country would have been converted to Islam.*" Here I recite the couplet from the Book 'Shiva Bavani' ending with the words:

Kashiji Ki Kalajati, Mathura masjid hoti

Shivaji jo na hote to Sunnat hoti Sabki

This was the delight of millions of people interested in knowing contemporary history and is a beautiful piece of literature. But Gandhiji would have none of it. Hindu-Muslim unity indeed!

(o) **Suhrawardy Patronised**—When the Muslim League refused to join the provisional Government which Lord Wavell invited Pandit Nehru to form; the League started a Council of direct action against any Government formed by Pandit Nehru. On the 15th of August 1946, a little more than two weeks before Pandit Nehru was to take office, there broke out in Calcutta an open massacre of the Hindus which continued for three days unchecked. The horrors of those days are described in the 'Statesman' newspaper of Calcutta. At that time it was considered that the Government which could permit such outrages on its citizens must be thrown out. There were suggestions that Mr. Suhrawardy's Government should be dismissed. But the socialist Governor refused to take up the administration under Section 93 of the

Government of India Act. Gandhiji however went to Calcutta and contracted a strange friendship with the author of these massacres. In fact he intervened on behalf of Suhrawardy and the Muslim League. During the three days that the massacre of Hindus took place, the police in Calcutta did not interfere for the protection of life or property; innumerable outrages were practised under the very eyes and nose of the guardians of law. But nothing mattered to Gandhiji. To him Suhrawardy was an object of admiration from which he could not be diverted and publicly described Suhrawardy as a 'Martyr'. No wonder two months later there was the most virulent outbreak of Muslim fanaticism in Noakhali and Tipperah, 30,000 Hindu women were forcibly converted according to a report of Arya Samaj. The total number of Hindus killed or wounded was three lacs. Not to say that the crores of rupees worth of property was looted and destroyed. Gandhiji then undertook, ostensibly alone, a tour of Noakhali District. It is well-known that Suhrawardy gave him protection wherever he went and even with that protection Gandhiji never ventured to enter Noakhali District. All these outrages, loss of life and property were done when Suhrawardy was the Prime Minister and to such a monster of inequity and communal poison, Gandhiji gave the unsolicited title of 'Martyr'.

(p) **Attitude towards Hindus and Muslim Princes**— Gandhiji's followers successfully humiliated the Jaipur, Bhavnagar and Rajkot States princes. They enthusiastically supported even a rebellion in Kashmir State against the Hindu prince. This attitude strangely enough contrasts with what Gandhiji did about the affairs in Muslim States. There was a Muslim League intrigue in Gwalior State; as a result of which the Maharaja was compelled to abandon the celebrations of the second millennium of the Vikram Calender four years ago. The Muslim agitation was based on pure communalism. The Maharaja is the liberal and impartial Ruler with a far sighted outlook. In a recent casual Hindu Muslim clash in Gwalior the Musalmans suffered some casualties

Gandhiji came down upon the Maharaja with a vitriolic attack which was wholly undeserved.

(q) **Gandhiji on Fast to Capacity**—In 1943 while Gandhiji was on fast to capacity and nobody was allowed to interview him on political affairs, only the nearest and the dearest had the permission to go and enquire of his health. Mr. C. Rajagopalachari smuggled himself into Gandhiji's room and hatched a plot of conceding Pakistan. Gandhiji allowed him to negotiate with Jinnah. Gandhiji later on discussed this matter for three weeks with Mr. Jinnah in the latter part of 1944 and offered Mr. Jinnah virtually what is now called Pakistan. Gandhiji went everyday to Mr. Jinnah's house. Flattered him, praised him, embraced him, but Mr. Jinnah could not be cajoled out of his demand for the Pakistan pound of flesh. Hindu Muslim unity was making progress in the negative direction.

(r) **Desai-Liaquat Agreement**—(i) In 1945 came the notorious Desai-Liaquat Agreement. It put one more, almost the last, nail on the coffin of the Congress as a National democratic body. Under that agreement, the late Mr. Bhulabhai Desai the then leader of the Congress Party in the Central Legislative Assembly at Delhi entered into an agreement with Mr. Liaquat Ali Khan, the League Leader in the Assembly to jointly demand a Conference with the British Government for the solution of the stalemate in Indian politics, which was growing since the beginning of the War. Mr. Desai was understood to have taken that step without consulting anybody of any importance in the Congress circle, as almost all the Congress leaders had been detained since the 'Quit India' Resolution in 1942. Mr. Desai offered equal representation to the Muslims with Congress at the said Conference and this was the basis on which the Viceroy was approached to convene the Conference. The then Viceroy Lord Wavell, flew to London on receipt of this joint request and brought back the consent of the Labour Government for holding the Conference. The official announcement in this behalf stupefied the country on account of its treachery to nationalism and democracy to which the Congress had become a party. Indian democracy was stabbed in the back and every principle of justice was violated. The Congress members quickly acquiesced in this monstrous proposal. The proposal however had, it was then revealed, the blessings of the Mahatma and was in fact made with his previous knowledge and consent. With the full agreement of the Congress party, 25% of the people of India were treated as if they were 50% and the 75% were brought down to the level of 50%. The Viceroy also laid down other conditions for holding the Conference. They were:

1. An unqualified undertaking on the part of the Congress and all political parties to support the war against Japan until the victory.
2. A coalition Government would be formed in which the Congress and the Muslims would each have five representatives. Besides there will be a representative of the depressed classes, of the Sikhs and other Minorities.
3. The 'Quit India' movement will unconditionally be withdrawn and the Congress leaders detained, in consequence of the movement would be released.
4. All measures of Administrative Reform will be within the four corners of the Government of India Act 1935.
5. The Governor General and the Viceroy shall retain the same constitutional position in the new setup as they had at that time i.e., the viceroy would remain the head of the new Government.
6. At the end of the war, the question of complete freedom will be decided through the machinery of the Constituent Assembly.
7. If these were accepted without any modification the Viceroy would reconstitute his Government with all portfolios to be held by Indians as per clause (2) above.
8. People who had only three years ago started the 'Quit India' movement for complete Independence and

exhorted the other people to 'Do or Die' in implementing the rebellion, quietly submitted to accept office under the leadership of a British Viceroy on the terms, and conditions laid down by him. The fact was that the 'Quit India' movement had failed, the Congress had no alternative programme and events were moving on whether the Congress party was ready for them or not. Mr. Jinnah was the only gainer from the collapse of the Congress. He obtained a great tactical advantage by the recognition of the Muslims' right to 50% representation in all future discussions. The two-nation theory and the demand for Pakistan received a fillip although the Conference failed without achieving the Hindu-Muslim unity.

(s) **Cabinet Mission Plan**—Early in the year 1946 the so-called Cabinet mission arrived in India. It consisted of the then Secretary of State for India now Lord Lawrence, Mr. Alexander, the Minister for War and Sir Stafford Cripps. Its arrival was heralded by a speech in Parliament by Mr. Atlee, the Prime Minister. Mr. Atlee announced in most eloquent terms the determination of the British Government to transfer power to India if the latter agreed upon common plan. The agreement was the pivot of the work of the mission but it was fatal. The Congress was honestly for a United India, but it was not outright in its conviction. It lacked firmness. Mr. Jinnah on the other hand demanded a divided India but he demanded it firmly. Between these two opposite demands, the mission found it impossible to bring about an agreement and after some further informal discussions with both, the mission announced its own solution on the 15th May 1946. It rejected and gave ten good reasons for that rejection but while firmly championing the unity of India the mission introduced Pakistan through the back-door. In paragraph 15 of the proposals the Mission introduced six conditions under which the British Government would be prepared to convene a Constituent Assembly invested with the right of framing a Constitution of Free India. Each of these six proposals were calculated to prevent the unity of India being maintained or full freedom being attained even if the Constituent Assembly was an elected body. The Congress party was so utterly exhausted by the failure of 'Quit India' that after some smoke-screen about its unflinching nationalism, it virtually submitted to Pakistan by accepting the Mission's proposals which made certain the dismemberment of India although in a roundabout manner. The Congress accepted the scheme but did not agree to form a Government, The long and short of it was that the Congress was called upon to form a Government and accept the whole scheme unconditionally. Mr. Jinnah denounced the British Government for treachery and started a direct action council of the Muslim League. The Bengal, the Punjab, the Bihar, the Bombay, and other places in various parts of India became scenes of bloodshed, arson, loot and rape on a scale unprecedented in 'history'. The overwhelming number of victims were Hindus. The Congress stood aghast but impotent and could not give any protection to the Hindus anywhere. The Governor General in spite of his powers to intervene under the Act of 1935 in case of a breach of peace and tranquility in India or in any part of it merely looked on and made no use of his obligations under the Act. A few lakhs of people were killed, many thousands of women and children were kidnapped and few of them have not yet been traced, thousands and thousands of women were raped, hundreds crores of property was looted, burnt or destroyed. The Mahatma, as far as ever before was far away from his goal of Hindu-Muslim unity.

(t) **Congress Surrenders to Jinnah**—By the following year the Congress Party abjectly surrendered to Mr. Jinnah at the point of bayonet and accepted Pakistan. What happened thereafter, is too well known. The thread running throughout this narrative is the increasing infatuation which Gandhiji developed for the Muslims. He uttered not one word of sympathy or comfort for millions of displaced Hindus; he had only one eye for humanity and that was for the Muslim humanity. The Hindus simply did not count to him. I was shocked by all these manifestations of Gandhian saintliness.

(u) **Ambiguous Statement about Pakistan**—In one of his articles, Gandhiji while nominally ostensibly opposed to Pakistan, openly declared that if the Muslims wanted Pakistan at any cost, there was nothing to prevent them from achieving it. Only the Mahatma could understand what that declaration meant. Was it a prophesy-or a declaration or disapproval of the demand for Pakistan?

(v) **Ill Advice to Kashmir Maharaja**—About Kashmir, Gandhiji again and again declared that Sheikh Abdullah should be entrusted the charge of the State and that the Maharaja of Kashmir should retire to Benares for no particular reason, other than that the Muslims formed the bulk of the Kashmir population. This also stands out in contrast with his attitude on Hyderabad where although the bulk of the population is Hindu, Gandhiji never called upon the Nizam to retire to Mecca.

(w) **Mountbatten vivisects India**—From August 15, 1946 onwards the private armies of the Muslim League began killing, devastating and destroying the Hindus wherever they could lay their hands on. Lord Wavell, the then Viceroy was undoubtedly greatly distressed at what was happening; but he did not use his powers under the Government of India Act of 1935 to prevent such a holocaust. Hindu blood began to flow from Bengal to Karachi with mild reactions in the Deccan. All the time from the 2nd September 1946 the so-called National Government consisting of two hybrid elements utterly reconcilable to each other was in office. The Muslim League members who were 50% of the Congress, did every thing in their power to make the working of a Coalition Government impossible. The Muslim League members did everything they could, to sabotage the coalition Government. The more they became disloyal and treasonable to the Government of which they formed a part, the greater was Gandhiji's infatuation for them. Lord Wavell had to resign as he could not bring about a settlement. He had some conscience which prevented him from supporting the partition of India. He had openly declared it to be unnecessary and undesirable. But his retirement was followed by the appointment of Lord Mountbatten. King Log was followed by King Stork. This Supreme Commander of the South East Asia was a purely military man and he had a great reputation for daring, and tenacity. He came to India with a determination to do or die, and he 'did', namely he vivisected India. He was more indifferent to human slaughter. Rivers of blood flowed under his very eyes and nose. He apparently was thinking that by the slaughter of Hindus so many opponents of his mission were killed, the greater the slaughter of the enemies greater the victory, and he pursued his aim relentlessly to its logical conclusion. Long before June 1948 the official date for handing over power, the wholesale murders of the Hindus had their full effect. The Congress which had boasted of its nationalism and democracy secretly accepted Pakistan literally at the point of the bayonet and abjectly surrendered to Mr. Jinnah. India was vivisected. One third of the Indian territory became foreign land to us from the 15th of August 1947. Lord Mountbatten came to be described in Congress circles as the greatest Viceroy and Governor General India had ever known. He had gifted ten months earlier than 30th June 1948 what is called Dominion status to vivisected India. This is what Gandhiji had achieved after thirty years of undisputed dictatorship and this is what the Congress Party calls 'Freedom'. Never in the history of the world has such slaughter been officially connived at, or the result, described as 'Freedom' and 'Peaceful Transfer of Power'. If what happened in India in 1946, 1947 and 1948 is to be called peaceful, one wonders what would be the violent. Hindu Muslim unity bubble was finally burst and a theocratic and communal State dissociated from everything that smacked of United India, was established with the consent of Nehru and his crowd. They have called it 'Freedom won by them at sacrifice'—Whose sacrifice ?

(x) **Gandhiji on Cow-Slaughter**—Gandhiji used to display a most vehement desire for the protection of the cow. But in fact he did no effort in that direction. On the contrary, in one of his post-prayer speeches, he has admitted his inability to support the demand for stopping cow-slaughter. An extract from his speech in this connection is reproduced below;

> Today Rajendra Babu informed me that he had received some fifty-thousand postcards, 20-30 thousand telegrams urging prohibition of cow-slaughter by law. In this connection I have spoken to you before also. After all why are so many letters and telegrams are sent to me. They have not served any purpose. No law prohibiting cow-slaughter in India can be enacted. How can I impose my will upon a person who does not wish voluntarily tc abandon cow-slaughter? India does not belong exclusively to the Hindus. Muslims, Parsees or Christians. All live here. The claim of the Hindus that India has become the land of the Hindus is totally incorrect. This land belongs to all who live here. I know an orthodox Vaishnava Hindu. He used to give beef soup to his child.

QUIT NOAKHALI OR DIE, GANDHI WARNS HINDUS

NEW DELHI, India, April 7 (AP) —Mohandas K. Gandhi, who has been attempting to insure communal peace in the Bengal and Bihar areas, said today religious strife in the troubled Noakhali section of Bengal seemed to call for Hindus to leave or perish "in the flames of fanaticism."

Meanwhile, a one-day strike of workers throughout Bombay Province appeared likely to be called by the Provincial Trade Union Congress to express sympathy with the two-week-old strike of 8,500 transport workers in the city of Bombay.

Mr. Gandhi halted his walking tour of Bengal and Bihar at the invitation of the new Viceroy, Viscount Mountbatten, for discussions

(y) **Removal of Tri-Colour Flag**—The tricolour flag with the Charkha on it was adopted by the Congress as the National Flag out of deference to Gandhiji. There were flag salutations on innumerable occasions. The flag was unfurled at every Congress meeting. It fluttered in hundreds at every session of National Congress. The *prabhat pheries* were never complete unless the flag was carried while the march was on. On the occasion of every imaginary or real success of the Congress party, public meetings, shops and private residences were decorated with that flag. If any Hindu attached any importance to Shivaji's Hindu Flag, *'Bhagva Zenda'* the flag which freed India from the Muslim domination, it was considered communal. Gandhiji's tricoloured flag never protected any Hindu woman from outrage or a Hindu temple from desecration, yet the late Bhai Parmanand was once mobbed by enthusiastic Congressmen for not paying homage to that flag. University students showed their patriotism by mounting that flag on University building. A Mayor of Bombay is believed to have lost his knighthood because his wife hoisted this flag on the Corporation building. Such was supposed to be the allegiance of the Congress people to their 'National Flag.' When the Mahatma was touring Noakhali and Tipper in 1946 after the beastly outrages on the Hindus, the flag was flying on his temporary hut. But when a Muslim came there and objected to the presence of the flag on his head, Gandhiji quickly directed its removal. All the reverential sentiments of millions of Congressmen towards that flag were affronted in a minute, because that would please an isolated Muslim fanatic and yet the great catholic Mahatma never got nearer to the so-called Hindu-Muslim unity.

PART III

GANDHIJI AND INDEPENDENCE

71. Some good number of people are labouring under the delusion that the freedom movement in India started with the advent of Gandhiji in 1914-15 and reached its consummation on the 15th August 1947, on the day it is said we attained Freedom under the leadership of the 'Father of the Nation.' In all the history, there was never a more stupendous fiction fostered by the cunning and believed by the credulous in this country for over a thousand years. Far from attaining freedom under his leadership, Gandhiji has left India torn and bleeding from a thousand wounds. There has always been a freedom movement alive in India which has never been suppressed. When the Mahratha Empire was finally subdued in 1818, British thought the forces of freedom were lying low for some time in some part of India but actually challenging the supremacy of the British so far as Northern India was concerned through the rise of Sikh power. And when by 1848 the Sikhs were defeated at Gujrat the rebellion of 1857 was being actively organised. It came with such suddenness and force and was so widespread that the British Imperialists began to shake in their shoes and more than once they seriously considered leaving India. The history of the great effort on the part of the Indian people to overthrow the British yoke has been vividly described in the pages of Veer Savarkar's *'War of Independence - 1857'*. By the time the British had fully regained control, the Indian National Congress was established once more to challenge the British domination. From 1885 the National urge for freedom began to assert itself, first

through constitutional methods, later by militant methods. The last one developed into armed- resistance which openly asserted itself through the bomb of Khudi Ram Bose in 1906.

72. Gandhiji arrived in India 1914-15. Nearly eight years earlier, the revolutionary movement had spread over a large part of India. The freedom movement had never died out. It had risen again like the Phoenix from its ashes. After the arrival of Gandhiji and his fads of truth and non-violence, the movement began to suffer eclipse. Thanks however to Subhash Chandra Bose and the revolutionaries in Maharashtra, Punjab and Bengal, that the movement continued to flourish, parallel to Gandhiji's rise to leadership after the death of Lokamanya Tilak.

73. Even the constitutional movements carried on by the moderates in the Congress registered some progress towards Freedom. In 1892 the British Government was obliged to extend the then Legislative Councils. This was followed by the Morley-Minto Reforms in 1909 when for the first time the elected representatives of the people secured the right to participate in the work of the Legislatures, both by their voices and their votes. Twelve years later, after the first World War, the Montague Chelmsford Reforms conceded partial Provincial Autonomy and also increased the number of elected members so as to give permanent non-official majority both at the Centre and in the Provinces. And in 1935, came the complete Provincial Autonomy and substantial Central responsibility which covered every subject except foreign policy, army, and to some extent Finance. Gandhiji had no love for Parliamentary bodies. He called them prostitutes, and always urged their boycott. Yet the constitutional progress upto 1935, little though it was, had been achieved. The Act of 1935 was of course seriously

defective. More especially because of the numerous and vexatious safeguards, granted to the British vested interests and the premium it placed on communalism.

74. There was further objection to it on the ground of the veto which it granted to the Governors and the 'Governor General.' Even then it is reasonably certain that if the Act had not been boycotted under Gandhiji's leadership, India would have long since reached the status of a Dominion which we are now supposed to be enjoying, after losing one-third of Indian territory.

75. I have already mentioned the revolutionary party which existed independent of the Congress. Amongst its sympathisers were many active Congressmen. This latter section was never reconciled to the yoke of Britain. During the First World War between 1914-1919 the Congress began to turn left and the terrorist movement outside was running parallel to the leftist party within. The Gadar Party was operating simultaneously in Europe and America in an effort to overthrow British Rule in India with the help of the Axis Powers. The 'Komagata Maru' incident is well known, and it is by no means clear that the 'Emden' incident on the Madras beach was not to the knowledge of the German Commander that India was seething with discontent. But from 1920 upwards, Gandhiji discouraged, put his foot down on the use of force although he himself carried on an active campaign for recruitment for soldiers to Britain only a few years earlier. The Rowlatt Report described at length the strength of the revolutionaries in India. From 1906 till 1918 one Britisher after another and his Indian stooges were shot dead by the revolutionary nationalists and the British authorities were trembling about their very existence. It was then that Mr. Montague came to this country as Secretary of State for India and promised the introduction

of responsibility; even he was only partially successful to stern the tide of revolutionary fervor. The Government of India Act 1919 was over-shadowed by the Jallianwalla Bagh Tragedy in which hundreds of Indians were shot dead by General Dwyer at a public meeting for the crime of holding a protest against the Rowlatt Act. Sir Michael O'Dwyer became notorious for callous and unscrupulous reprisals against those who had denounced the Rowlatt Act. Twenty years later he had to pay for it, when Udham Singh shot him dead in London. Madanlal Dhingra, Kanhere, Bhagat Singh, Rajguru Sukhdeo, Chandrashekhar Azad were the living examples of protest by Indian youth against the alien yoke. They had unfurled and held aloft the flag of Independence, some of them long before Gandhiji's name was heard of and even when he was accepted the leader of the constitutional movement of the Indian National Congress.

76. I had already stated that the revolutionary movement beginning in Bengal and Maharashtra later on reached Punjab. The young men associated with it did not come from the riff-raff of society. They were educated, cultural men belonging to most respectable families having high social status in private life. They sacrificed lives of comfort and ease at the altar of the liberty of the Motherland. They were the martyrs whose blood became the cementing force of the Indian Independence. Lokmanya Tilak built on it and the Mahatma got advantage of the accumulated momentum of this movement. It is my firm conviction that each stage of constitutional progress between 1909 and 1935 became possible as a result of the revolutionary forces working in the background.

77. Moderate opinion condemned the revolutionary violence. Gandhiji publicly denounced it day after day on every platform and through the press. There is however

little doubt that the overwhelming mass of the people gave their silent but whole-hearted support to the vanguard of the armed resistance working for national freedom. The theory of the revolution is that a nation always tries to wage a war on its alien conquerors. It owes no allegiance to the conqueror, and the very fact of its domination carries with it a notice to him that he may be overthrown any moment. The judgments passed on the armed resistance by a subject people to the foreign master, on the principle of allegiance of the citizen to his State is altogether beside the mark. And the more the Mahatma condemned the use of force in the country's battle for freedom, the more popular it became. This fact was amply demonstrated at the Karachi session of the Congress in March 1931; in the teeth of Gandhiji's opposition a resolution was passed in the open session admiring the courage and the spirit of sacrifice of Bhagat Singh when he threw the bomb in the Legislative Assembly in 1929. Gandhiji never forgot this defeat and when a few months later, Mr. Hotson, the Acting Governor of Bombay was shot at by Gogate, Gandhiji returned the charge at an All-India Congress Committee meeting and asserted that the admiration expressed by the Karachi Congress for Bhagat Singh was at the bottom of Gogate's action in shooting at Hotson. This astounding statement was challenged by Subhash Chandra Bose in the meeting of the same A.I.C.C. He immediately came into disfavour with Gandhiji. To sum up, the share of revolutionary youth in the fight for Indian Freedom, is by no means negligible and those who talk of India's freedom having been secured by Gandhiji are not only ungrateful lot but are trying to write the false history. The true history of India from 1895 onwards for the freedom of the country will never be written so long as Indian affairs are in charge of the Gandhian Group. The memorable share of the youth will be kept back. It is nevertheless true that they have played a noble and creditable part.

78. It were not merely those who advocate the use of force in the freedom battle whom Gandhiji opposed. Even those who held political views radically different from his one, and those who did not accept his nostrums, whom Gandhiji made them the target of displeasure. An outrageous example of his dislike of people with whom he did not agree is the case of Subhash Chandra Bose. So far as I am aware, no protest was ever made by Gandhiji against the deportation of Subhash for six years and Bose's election to the Presidential chair of the Haripura Congress was rendered possible only after he had personally disavowed any sympathy for violence. In actual practice however Subhash never toed the line that Gandhiji wanted, during his term of office. And yet, Subhash was so popular in the country that against the declared wishes of Gandhiji in favour of Dr. Pattabhi, he was elected president of the Congress for a second time with a substantial majority even from the Andhra Desha, the province of Dr. Pattabhi himself. This upset Gandhiji beyond endurance and he expressed his anger in the Mahatmic manner full of concentrated venom by stating that the success of Subhash was his defeat and not that of Dr. Pattabhi. Even after this declaration, his anger against Subhash Bose was not gratified. Out of sheer cursedness, he absented himself from the Tripura Congress session, staged a rival show at Rajkot by a wholly mischievous fast, and not until Subhash was overthrown from the Congress *gaddi* that the venom of Gandhiji became completely gutted.

79. This incident of the re-election of Subhash to the Congress crown and of his eventual expulsion from

residential office, is an indication of the hypocrisy with which the Mahatma controlled and repudiated the Congress as and when he liked. He had repeatedly stated after 1934 with a great show of detachment, that he was a four anna member of the Congress Party and he had nothing to do with it. But when Subhash was elected for a second time, Gandhiji completely lost his balance and furnished the best proof that he had interfered with that election from the very inception in favour of Dr. Pattabhi; it is a proof of his keen and engrossing interest in the rivalries and petty squabbles within the Congress at every stage while professing to be not even a member of that body.

80. When the 'Quit India' Movement was launched by the Congress, on 8th August 1942 on the initiative of Gandhiji, most of its leaders were quickly arrested by Government before they could make any start and the movement though it was non-violent, was nipped in the bud. There was another section in the Congress itself which went underground. The latter were not overanxious to follow the Gandhian technique and to go to jail. On the contrary, they wanted to avoid going to jail as long as possible and in the meantime do the maximum damage to Government by cutting communications, committing arson, loot and other acts of violence, not excluding murder. The statement of Gandhiji exhorting the people to 'Do or Die' was interpreted by that section as giving them full scope for all kinds of obstruction and sabotage. In fact they did everything to paralyse the war effort of Government to the fullest extent. Police Thanas were burnt, postal communications were violently interrupted. In north Bihar and other places, nearly 900 railway stations were either burnt or destroyed and the administration was almost brought to a standstill for some time.

81. These activities were directly opposed to the Congress creed of non-violence and to the satyagrah technique. Gandhiji could neither support nor oppose these latter activities. If he supported them, his creed of non-violence would stand exposed. If he opposed them publicly he would become unpopular with the masses who did not care one brass button whether the expulsion of the British from India was accomplished by violence or non-violence. In fact, the 'Quit India' campaign was known more for its acts of violence on the part of Congress supporters than for anything else. Gandhiji's non-violence had died within few weeks of starting the 'Quit India' campaign while the violence that was being committed under that name found no favour with him. The Gandhian point of view was entirely absent from the activities of the Congress party and its supporters within a few weeks of the 8th August 1942. Nowhere was non-violence either preached or practised as the supporters of the campaign were, in the words of Gandhiji himself, prepared to 'Do or Die'. It was only when Lord Linlithgow in his correspondence with Gandhiji in 1943 categorically challenged him to own or disown the violence on the part of the supporters of the 'Quit India' campaign, that Gandhiji was forced to condemn that violence. Whatever embarrassment, damage, inconvenience and harm was done to the war efforts, was the result of the violent activities of the Congress supporters and not the so-called non-violence of the Mahatma. Non-violence had completely failed; violence to some extent appeared to have succeeded, but Gandhiji had to denounce it from the jail. The revolutionary struggle for independence was thus discouraged by Gandhiji while his own strategy had completely collapsed soon after the 8th August 1942.

82. By this time, Mr. Subhash Chandra Bose, who had mysteriously escaped from India early in January 1942 had already arrived in Japan after reaching Berlin through Afghanistan. The way in which Mr. Subhash Chandra Bose escaped from Calcutta in January 1941 and the hardships and sufferings which he had to undergo on his way through the Indian Frontier to Kabul and thence to Berlin are vividly described by Mr. Uttam Chand in his book *'When Bose was Ziauddhin'*. The courage and tenacity with which Bose faced all privations, all dangers, all difficulties, eventually reaching Berlin made the most thrilling and romantic reading. By the time of the arrival of the Cripps Mission in India in 1942 he had already reached Japan and was organising an invasion of India. Before Subhash left Germany, Hitler had honoured him with the title of His Excellency. On reaching Japan he found the Japanese ready to assist him against the British in the invasion of the country. Japan had already joined the war on the side of the axis by the attack on the Pearl Harbour in America; Germany had declared war on Russia. Britain and France in turn, had declared war on Italy, Germany and Japan. In Japan, Federated Malaya States, Burma and in other parts of the Far East, Subhash received most enthusiastic welcome and immense support from the Indians settled there.

83. The Japanese had intensified their war effort and occupied Burma, Dutch East Indies, Federated Malaya States and the whole of the Far East including the Andaman Islands. Subhash Chandra Bose was thereby abled to start a provisional Indian Republican Government on Indian territory. By 1944 he was equipped to start an invasion of India with the help of the Japanese. Pandit Nehru declared that if Subhash Chandra Bose came into India with the support of the Japanese he would fight

Subhash. Early in 1944, Japanese and the Indian National Army organised by Subhash were thundering at the gates of India and they had already entered Manipur State and some part of the Assam Frontier. The I.N.A. consisted of volunteers from the Indian population of the Far East and of those Indians who had deserted to the I.N.A. from the Japanese prisons. That the campaign eventually failed was no fault of Subhash; his men fought like the Trojans. But his difficulties were far too great and his army was not sufficiently equipped with modern armaments. The I.N.A. had no aeroplanes and their supply-line was weak. Many died of starvation and illness as there was no adequate medical treatment available to them. But the spirit which Subhash engendered in them was wonderful. He was lovingly described by them as 'Netaji' Subhash Chandra Bose, and they had adopted the slogan of 'Jai Hind' under his leadership.

84. Gandhiji was opposed to Subhash Chandra Bose's invasion of India. Nehru was opposed to him because he did not approve of Bose's support to the Japanese invader. But whatever differences may have existed between Bose and the other Indian leaders, there was no doubt that Subhash was loved more than any other leader because of his single-handed effort to destroy British imperialism. If Subhash had been alive and had entered India in 1945 after the defeat of the Japanese army, the whole Indian population would, like one man, have been behind him and given him the most affectionate welcome. But Gandhiji was again more lucky. Lokmanya Tilak died in 1920 and Gandhiji became the unchallenged leader. Success of Subhash Chandra would have a crushing defeat for Gandhiji, but luck was again on his side and Subhash Chandra died outside India. It then became easy for the Congress party to profess love and admiration for Subhash

Chandra Bose and the I.N.A. and even to defend some of its officers and men in the Great State Trial in 1946 in this very Red Fort. They even adopted 'Jai Hind' as the slogan which Subhash had introduced in the Far East. They traded on the name of Subhash and the I.N.A. The two issues which led them to victory during the election in 1945-46 were their pretended affection for the I.N.A. and their hypocritical homage to Subhash's memory. Moreover the Congress party had promised they were opposed to Pakistan and would resist it at all costs. On these two assurances, they treated the I.N.A. with scant courtesy and of course they succumbed to Pakistan in breach of their promise.

85. All this time the Muslim League was carrying on treasonable activities, disturbing the peace and tranquility of India carrying on a murderous campaign against the Hindus. Lord Wavell and Lord Mountbatten looked on entirely unconcerned. The Congress would not venture to condemn or to stop these wholesale massacres in pursuit of its policy of appeasement at all costs. Gandhiji suppressed everything which did not fit in with his pattern of public activities. I am therefore surprised, when claims are made over and over again, that the winning of the freedom was due to Gandhiji. My own view is that constant pandering to the Muslim League was not the way to winning freedom. It only created a Frankenstein monster, which ultimately devoured its own creator swallowing one-third of Indian territory, and permanently stationing a hostile, censorious, unfriendly and aggressive neighbour on what was once Indian territory. About the winning of Swaraj and freedom, I maintain the Mahatama's contribution was negligible. But I am prepared to give him a place as a sincere patriot. His teachings however have produced opposite result and his leadership has stultified

the nation. In my opinion S.C. Bose is the supreme hero and martyr of modern India. He kept alive and fostered the revolutionary mentality of the masses, advocating all honourable means, including the use of force when necessary for the liberation of India. Gandhiji and his crowd of self-seekers tried to destroy him. It is thus entirely incorrect to represent the Mahatma as the architect of Indian Independence.

86. The real cause of the British leaving this country is threefold and it does not include the Gandhian method. The aforesaid triple forces are—

(i) The movements of the Indian Revolutionaries right from 1857 to 1932, i.e. upto the death of Chandra Shekhar Azad at Allahabad. Next is the movement of revolutionary character not that of Gandhian type in the countrywide rebellion of 1942, but an armed revolt put up by Subhash Chandra Bose, the result of which, a spread of the revolutionary mentality in the Military Forces of India are the real dynamic factors that have shattered the very foundation of the British Rule in India. And all these effective efforts to freedom were opposed by Gandhiji.

(ii) A good deal of credit must be given to those who, imbibed with a spirit of patriotism, fought with the Britishers strictly on constitutional lines on the Assembly floors and made a notable progress in Indian politics. The view of this section was to take a maximum advantage of whatever we have obtained and to fight further on! This section was generally represented by late Lokmanya Tilak, Mr. N.C. Kelkar, Mr. C.R. Das, Mr. Vithhalbhai Patel brother of Hon'ble Sardar Patel, Pandit Malviya, Bhai Parmanand, and during last ten years by prominent Hindu Sabha leaders. The sacrifices and intelligence of this school of men was also ridiculed by Gandhiji himself and his followers by calling them as job hunters or power seekers. Although they often ultimately resorted to the same methods.

(iii) There is also one more, but nonetheless important reason for the Britishers which made them part with power. That is the advent of Labour Government and an overthrow of Mr. Churchill, superimposed by the frightful economic conditions and the financial bankruptcy to which the war had reduced Britain.

87. So long as Gandhian method was in ascendance, frustration was the only inevitable result. He had throughout opposed every spirited revolutionary, radical and vigorous individual or group, and constantly boosted his charkha, non-violence and truth. The charkha after 34 years of the best efforts of Gandhiji, had only led to the expansion of the machine-run textile industry by over 200 per cent. It is unable even now to clothe even one per cent of the nation. As regards non-violence, it was absurd to expect 40 crores of people to regulate their lives on such a lofty plane and it broke down most conspicuously in 1942. As regards truth, the least I can say is that the truthfulness of the average Congressman is by no means of a higher order than that of the man in the street and that very often it is untruth in reality masked by a thin veneer of pretended truthfulness.

Apte, Veer Savarker, Nathuram, Vishnu Karkare (sitting from left to right) Kistya, Gopal Godse, Madan Lal, Badge (standing from left to right)

An affidavit submitted by Savarkar in the Bombay High Court sites this picture as taken without his consent on 11 May 1948.

PART-IV

FRUSTRATION OF AN IDEAL

88. Really speaking the idea of Hindu-Muslim unity which Gandhiji had put forward when he entered Indian Politics, came to an end from the moment the Pakistan was established. The Muslim league was opposed to regard India as one whole nation; and over and over again they had stated with great obstinacy, that they were not Indians. The Hindu Muslim unity which Gandhiji himself had put forward many a time was not of this type. What he wanted was that they both should take part in the struggle for independence as comrades. That was his idea of Hindu-Muslim unity. The Hindus followed Gandhiji's advice. The Muslims on every occasion, disregarded it and indulged in such behaviour as would be insulting to the Hindus, and at last, it has culminated in the vivisection and division of the country.

89. The mutual relations of Gandhiji and Mr. Jinnah are also worthy of note. When Mr. Jinnah, who once was an ardent nationalist became rank communalist from 1920 onward, since then he put forward one evident and clear fact that it was his intention to look to the interest of the Muslim community and that the Muslims should not at all rely upon the Congress and Congress leaders. The Muslims should not support the fight for freedom along with the Congress. Mr. Jinnah had also openly demanded Pakistan. He has preached these doctrines quite openly. He has deceived no one as far as principles are concerned. His the behaviour of an open enemy. He could talk of vivisecting this country with ease and wholly unfettered tongue.

90. Gandhiji had seen and called upon Mr. Jinnah many a time. Every time he had to plead to him as "brother Jinnah'. He even offered to him the premiership of the whole of India; but there was, not a single occasion on which Mr. Jinnah had shown any inclination even to co-operate.

91. Gandhiji's inner voice, his spiritual power and his doctrine of non-violence of which so much is made of, crumbled before Mr. Jinnah's iron will and proved to be powerless.

92. Having known that with his spiritual powers he could not influence Mr. Jinnah, Gandhiji should have either changed his policy or admitted his defeat and given way to others of different political views to deal with Mr. Jinnah and the Muslim League. But Gandhiji was not honest enough to do that. He could not forget his egoism or self, even for national interest. There was, thus, no scope left for the practical politics while the great blunders—blunders as big as the Himalayas—were being committed.

93. Constantly for nearly one year after the horrible Noakhali massacre, our nation was, as if, bathing in the pool of blood. The Muslims indulged in horrible and dreadful massacre of humanity followed by reactions from Hindus in some parts. The attacks of Hindus on Muslims in the East Punjab, Bihar or Delhi, were simply acts of reaction. It is not that Gandhiji did not know that the basic cause of these reactions was the outrages on Hindus by the Muslims in the Muslim majority Provinces. But still Gandhiji went on condemning strongly such actions of Hindus only, and the Congress Government went to the extent of threatening to even bombard the Hindus in Bihar to check their discontent and reactions against Muslims which was mainly due to the Muslim outbursts and atrocities in Noakhali and elsewhere. Gandhiji had

often advocated during the course of his prayers that the Hindus in India should treat the Muslims with respect and generosity even though the Hindus and Sikhs in Pakistan may be completely massacred, and though Mr. Suhrawardy may be the leader of the goondas, he should be allowed to move about freely and safely in Delhi. This will be evident from extracts given below from Gandhiji's post-prayer speeches:

(a) 'We should with a cool mind reflect when we are being swept away. Hindus should never be angry against the Muslims even if the latter might make up their minds to undo even their existence. If they put all of us to the sword, we should court death bravely, may they, even rule the world, we shall inhabit the world. At least we should never fear death. We are destined to be born and die; then why need we feel gloomy over it. 'If all of us die with a smile on our lips, we shall enter a new life: We shall originate a new Hindustan'. (6th April 1947).

(b) The few gentlemen from Rawalpindi who called upon me today were sturdy, brave and absorbed in business. I advised them to remain calm. After all God is great. There is no place where God does not exist. Mediate on Him and take His name; everything will be all right. They asked me what about those who still remained in Pakistan. I asked them why they came here (in Delhi). Why they did not die there? I still hold on to the belief one should stick to the place where we happen to give even if we are cruelly treated and even killed. Let us die if the people kill us; but we should die bravely with the name of God on our tongue. Even if our men are killed, why should we feel angry with anybody, you should realise that even if they are killed they have had a good and proper end. May the heaven make us all so. May God send us the same way. This is what we should pray heartily for. I will advise you (and issue) as I did to the residents of Rawalpindi, that they should go there and meet the Sikhs and Hindu refugees, tell them politely to return to their places in Pakistan unaided either by Police or the Military'. (23rd September 1947).

(c) 'Not one of those who have died in Punjab is going to return. In the end we too have to go there. It is true that they were murdered but then some others die of cholera or due to others causes. He who is born must die. If those killed have died bravely they have not lost anything but earned something. But what to do with those who have slaughtered people, is a big question. One may concede that to err is human. A human being is a bundle of errors. In Punjab our protection is due to them (British troops). But is this protection? I want even if a handful of persons protect themselves, they should not be afraid of death. After all the killers will be none other than our Muslim brothers. Will our brothers cease to be our brothers after change of their religion? And do we not act like them? What thing we left undone with women in Bihar.'

94. Gandhiji needs have taken into consideration that the desire for reprisals springing up in the Hindu mind was simply a natural reaction. Thousands of Hindus in the Muslim Provinces were being massacred simply because of the fault of their being Hindus, and our Government was quite unable to render these unfortunate people any help or protection. Could it be in any way unnatural if the waves of sorrow and grief of the Hindus in those Provinces should redound on the mind and hearts of the Hindus in other Provinces? It was not at all unnatural, for these reactions were only the signs of warm humanity. Only with the sole object of redressing the woes and calamities of their fellow brothers in those provinces and giving them protection, that the retaliation against the Muslims was resorted to, as the Hindus believed that was the only way by which the atrocities of the Muslims could be checked. When the people (Hindus) noticed and realised that the Indian Union Government was unable to afford any protection to their brethren residing in Pakistan, they thought of taking the law in their own hands. The retaliatory actions taken by the Hindus in

Bihar and elsewhere were the inevitable outcome of the revulsion left by the Hindus at the shocking atrocities in other provinces. Such a feeling at times also is as spiritual and natural as that of kindness.

95. Many a great revolution has been successful only by the idea of this sort of feeling of acute discontent against the misdeeds of the rulers. It would be quite impossible to put an end to the governance of the Society by the wicked, had it not been for such feelings of discontent, retaliation and revenge springing up against the wicked Dictators. The events of ancient history as depicted in Ramayana and Mahabharat, or the more modern wars of England and America against Germany and Japan do indicate the same sort of action and reaction. It may be either good or bad, but such is the human nature.

96. Looking at from the point of view of the Indian politics, I have already shown in my narration elsewhere, how Gandhiji had strongly opposed several efforts made for winning the freedom of the country. There was no consistency in his own political policy in particular, or in his behaviour at the time of the last war was quite unthinkable.

97. He first gave out the principle that no help should be given by India to the war between England and Germany. 'WAR MEANT VIOLENCE AND HOW COULD I HELP' was the saying. But the wealthy companions and followers of Gandhiji enormously added to their wealth by undertaking contracts from the Government for the supply of materials for war. It is needless for me to mention names but all know the wealthy personalities like Birla, Dalmia, Walchand Hirachand, Nanjibhai Kalidas, etc. Gandhiji and his Congress colleagues have been much helped by everyone of them. Gandhiji never refused to

accept the money offered by these wealthy people although it was obtained from this blood-filled war. Nor did he prevent these wealthy people from carrying out their contracts with the Government for the supply of the materials for war. Not only that, Gandhiji had given his consent to taking up the contract for supplying blankets to the army from the Congress Khadi Bhandar.

98. Gandhiji's release from jail in 1944 was followed by the release of other leaders also, the Government had to be assured by the Congress leaders of their help in the war against Japan. Gandhiji not only did not oppose this but actually supported the Government proposal.

99. In Gandhiji's politics, there was no place for consistency of ideas and reasons. Truth was what Gandhiji only could define. His politics was supported by old superstitious beliefs such as the power of the soul, the inner voice, the fast, the prayer, and the purity of mind.

100. Gandhiji had once said:

Freedom Got from Non-violence A Thousand Years Later, Is Preferable to the Freedom got today by Violence.

Whether he acted as he said, or whether his actions and sayings were diametrically opposed to each other can be inferred to some extent from the example cited above.

101. A recent example of the inconsistency of his doctrine of non-violence is worth being noted in particular The problem of Kashmir followed very closely that of Pakistan. Pakistan had begun a dreadful invasion to conquer and gulp down the Kashmir. The Maharaja of Kashmir had asked for help from the Nehru Government, and the latter in return agreed to do so on the condition that Sheikh Abdullah would be made the Chief Administrator. On every important matter Pt. Nehru had consulted Gandhiji. There was every chance of partiality

being done, Kashmir being the birth-place of Pt. Nehru. And to give no way to this partiality, Pt. Nehru consulted Gandhiji about sending Military help to Kashmir and it was only on the consent of Gandhiji that Pt. Nehru sent troops for the protection and defence of Kashmir. Pandit Nehru himself has told this in one of his speeches.

102. Our political leaders knew from the very beginning that the invasion of Kashmir by the raiders was supported by Pakistan. And it was therefore, evident that sending help to the Kashmir meant waging war directly against Pakistan. Gandhiji himself was opposed to the war with arms, and he has told this to the entire world again and again. But he gave his consent to Pt. Nehru to send army in Kashmir. The only conclusion that could be drawn from what is happening in Kashmir is that, today after the attainment of freedom for the partitioned India, that under Gandhiji's blessings, our Government has resorted to the war where man-killing machinery is being used.

103. Had Gandhiji a firm belief in the doctrine of non-violence, he should have made a suggestion for sending Satyagrahis instead of the armed troops and tried the experiment. Orders should have been issued to send '*Takalis*' in place of rifles and 'Spinning wheels' (*i.e. Charkhas*) instead of the guns. It was a golden opportunity for Gandhiji to show the power of his Satyagraha by following his precept as an experiment at the beginning of our freedom.

104. But Gandhiji did nothing of the sort. He had begun a new war by his own will, at the very beginning of the existence of Free India. What does this inconsistency mean? Why did Gandhiji himself so violently trample down the doctrine of non-violence, he had championed? To my mind, the reason for his doing so is quite obvious; and it is

that this war is being fought for Sheikh Abdullah. The administrative power of Kashmir was going in the hands of Muslims and for this reason and this reason alone did Gandhiji consent to the destruction of the raiders by Armed Forces. Gandhiji was reading the dreadful news of Kashmir war, while at the same time fasting to death only because a few Muslims could not live safely in Delhi. But he was not bold enough to go on fast in front of the raiders of Kashmir, nor had he the courage to practise Satyagraha against them. All his fasts were to coerce Hindus.

105. I thought it is rather a very unfortunate thing, that in the present 20th Century such a hypocrite should have been regarded as the leader of the All India politics. The mind of this Mahatma was not affected by the attacks on the Hindus in Hyderabad State. This Mahatma never asked the Nizam of Hyderabad to abandon his throne. If the Indian politics proceeded in this way under the guiding dominance of Gandhiji, even the preservation of freedom obtained today—even in partitioned India would be impossible. These thoughts arose in my mind again and again and it was full with them. As the above incidents were taking place, Gandhiji's fast for the Hindu-Muslim unity was announced on 13th January 1948, and then I lost nearly all my control on my feelings.

106. For the last four years, I had been working as the Editor of a daily newspaper, and even before this period, I have spent most of my time in the service of the public. As such therefore, I was in a habit of being in touch with all the Indian political developments.

107. I was fully aware of the idea of the mutual relations among the three political bodies—the Muslim League, the Congress and the Hindu Mahasabha. The Muslim League had always dubbed the Congress as a

Hindu organisation, but the Congress leaders were ashamed of being called part of a Hindu body. The Congressmen felt abused when called 'Communal'.

108. Really speaking, if any institution were to look to the interests of a particular community without hindering the growth of national spirit, why should one use the word 'communal' in the sense of an abuse to that institution? It would be proper if an institution seeking the interests of any particular community by destroying the very essence of the national spirit were to be abused as being a selfish 'Communal minded' body. But the Congress has no such discretion. The Congress has styled both the Muslim League and the Hindu Mahasabha as 'Communal bodies' using the word 'Communal' as an expression of abuse. But the thing to be specially noted is that while the Congress has yielded to every demand of the Muslim League, it has not taken due notice of even the purely national policy of the Hindu Mahasabha and has carried on propaganda of distortion against Hindu Mahasabha and its leaders.

109. When the Congress recognised the Muslim League as representing the Muslim Community viewed from logical point of view it would not have been out of place to recognise the Hindu Mahasabha as representing the Hindus, or, at least the Congress should openly have declared that it would look to the interests of the Hindus. But the Congress never did that. As a result of all this, in spite of the existence of a very powerful body such as the Muslim League looking after the interests of the Muslims, a few Muslims who were still the members of the Congress, also looked after the Muslim interest; whereas there was none to look after the Hindu interest as such. The Congress which derided the Hindu Mahasabha by calling it 'Communal' took part in the conference of leaders convened

by H.E. Lord Wavell at Simla, and accepted the principle of 50 per cent representation of the Muslims. Not only that, but at the instance of Gandhiji the Congress leaders were prepared to be recognised as representatives of Caste Hindus. This position taken by the Congress was the most hideously communal one being entirely the outcome of the Muslim-appeasing policy adopted by it.

110. Was the ideal of freedom and independence of India, torn by vivisection, before the Congress, on the foundation of which our great national, intelligent and sacrificing leaders laboured assiduously by keeping before them the ideal of the freedom of the whole nation, sacrificed even their lives for their ideal of the achievement of complete democracy, and tried for the mutual co-operation among the major and minor communities of this vast country and in the freedom fight of which the parts of Punjab, Bengal, Sind, and N.W.F. Province, which now form the Pakistan, were in no way less prominent than any other part of India? So also, could those patriots with their ideal of the freedom of the whole of Bharatkhand, who were, though outside the Congress, but were in the forefront of the revolution who either gladly went to the gallows or passed their days out of their motherland as exiles, or were rotting in the dark cells of the Andamans; dream of freedom as envisaged in the freedom granted to the country by vivisection? Is it proper that the reward for their incomparable sacrifices should be in the establishment of a State founded upon blind and fanatic religious faith in one part of the country?

111. But the Congress under the leadership of Gandhiji commenced its surrender to the Muslims, right from the time the 14 demands of Mr. Jinnah were made till the establishment of the Pakistan. Is it not a deplorable

sight for people to see the Congress celebrate the occasion of the establishment of a Dominion Government in the rest of country shattered and vivisected by the Pakistan in the East and West and with the pricking thorn of Hyderabad in its midst. On seeing this downfall of the Congress under the dominance of Gandhiji, I am reminded of the well known verse of Raja Bhartrihari to the effect:

शिरः शार्वं स्वर्गात्पशुपति शिरस्तः क्षितिधरं
महीध्रादुत्तुङ्गादवनिमवनेश्चापि जलधिम्।
अथो गङ्गा सेयं पदमुपगता स्नोकमयथा
विवेक भ्रष्टानां भवति विनिपातः शतमुखः।।

(भर्तृहरिः नीति शतक नौ)

(The Ganges has fallen from the Heavens on the head of Shiva, thence on the Himalayas, thence on the earth, and thence in the sea. In this manner, down and down she went and reached a very low stage. Truly it is said that indiscriminate persons deteriorate to the low position in a hundred ways.)

Seen in the Picture is Judge Atma Charan (in circle), Vishnu Karkare, Narayan Apte, Nathuram Godse, Gopal Godse, Veer Savarkar, etc.

PART-V

Climax of Anti-national Appeasement

112. The day on which I decided to remove Gandhiji from the political stage, it was clear to me that personally I shall be lost to everything that could be mine. I am not a moneyed person but I did have a place of honour and respect amongst those known as middle class society. I have been in the public life of my Province and the service that I have been able to render so far has given me a place of honour and respect amongst my people. Ideas of culture and civilisation are not strange to me. I had in my view before me some schemes of constructive work to be taken in hand in my future life and I felt I had enough strength and enthusiasm to undertake them and carry them out successfully. I have maintained robust health and I do not suffer from any bodily defect and I am not addicted to any vice. Although I myself am not a much-learned man, I have a great regard and admiration for the learned.

113. Since the year 1929-30 when the Congress launched its first campaign of the Civil Disobedience Movement, I entered the life of a public worker. I was merely a student then. The lectures related to this movement and the accounts thereof published in the newspapers had greatly impressed me and I resolved to join the movement and take the career of a public worker. Just after this, the movement was over the problems related to Muslims assumed grave appearance and a movement to bring about the unification of the Hindus was being taken in hand more intensely, by the Hindu Sabha leaders like Dr. Moonje, Bhai Parmanandji, Pandit Madan Mohan Malaviya as also by some leaders of the

Arya Samaj and by the workers of the Rashtriya Swayam Sevak Sangh. The question of Communal Award was under hot discussion amongst all the political bodies and it is also noteworthy to mention here that in the Session of the Hindu Mahasabha which was held at Poona in the year 1935, it was decided to contest the elections for legislatures against the Congress as the views of the latter were unfairly in favour of the Muslims and detrimental to the Hindus. This contest against the Congress was decided by the Hindu Mahasabha under the auspices of the late Pandit Madan Mohan Malviya who was also a veteran leader of the Congress.

114. About the year 1932 late Dr. Hedgewar of Nagpur founded the Rashtriya Swayam Sevak Sangh in Maharashtra. His oration greatly impressed me and I joined the Sangha as a volunteer thereof. I am one of those volunteers of Maharashtra who joined the Sangha in its initial stage. I also worked for a few years on the intellectual side in the Province of Maharashtra. Having worked for the upliftment of the Hindus I felt it necessary to take part in the political activities of the country for the protection of the just rights of Hindus. I therefore left the Sangha and joined the Hindu Mahasabha.

115. In the year 1938, I led the first batch of volunteers who marched into the territory of the Hyderabad State when the passive resistance movement was started by the Hindu Mahasabha, with a demand for Responsible Government in the State. I was arrested and sentenced to one year's imprisonment. I have a personal experience of the uncivilized, nay barbarous rule of Hyderabad, and have undergone the corporal punishment of dozens of cane lashes for the offence of singing the 'Vande Mataram' song at the time of prayer.

116. In the year 1943 the Bihar Government had issued a proclamation prohibiting the holding of the Hindu Mahasabha Session at Bhagalpur. The Mahasabha resolved to defy this ban as it felt that the action of the Government was unjust and illegal. The session was held in spite of all the precautions taken by the Government for its prevention. I took a leading part in the preparation for the session keeping myself underground for nearly a month. During this period while reading newspapers I have come across items of news appreciating my work, I have also heard people expressing their approval of my part in public life. By nature I am not a person of violent temperament. The approver Badge in his deposition at page 225 has stated that I took out a knife to stab Mr. Bhopatkar. This statement is totally false. Mr. Bhopatkar is at present leading the lawyers defending the accused. Had I made any such assault as described by the approver could he have come forward to render us assistance in our defence? If that alleged incident were true, I should have least thought of taking the help of Mr. Bhopatkar.

117. Those, who personally know me, take me as a person of quiet temperament. But when the top-rank leaders of the Congress with the consent of Gandhiji divided and tore the country—which we consider as a deity of worship—my mind became full with the thoughts of direful anger.

I wish to make it clear that I am not an enemy of the Congress. I have always regarded that body as the premier institution which has worked for the political uplift of the country. I had, and have, my differences with its leaders. This will be clearly seen from my letter addressed to Veer Savarkar on 28th February 1938 (RX D/30) which is in my hand and signed by me and I admit its contents.

118. There was no enmity between Gandhiji and myself on any personal grounds. To those who speak of Gandhiji's honest motive in supporting Pakistan, I have only to say that I have nothing but the purest interest of our nation at my heart in taking the extreme step against the person of Gandhiji, who was the most responsible and answerable person for the terrible event culminating in the creation of Pakistan. I could foresee the result of my action against the life of Gandhiji and did very well realise that the moment the people come to know about it they would change their view about me in spite of the circumstances. My status and honour in the society and the sympathies which the people entertained for me will be smashed completely. I fully realised that I would be looked upon as the most despicable fellow in the society.

119. I had a fare idea about fiery attacks that would be launched against me in the Press. But I never thought that I could be cowed down by the fire poured against me by the Press. For, had the Indian Press impartially criticised the anti-national policy carried on by Gandhiji and had they impressed upon the people that the interest of the nation was far greater than the whim of any individual howsoever great he may be, Gandhiji and his followers could never have dared concede Pakistan to the Muslims as easily as has been done. The Press had displayed such weakness and submission to the High Command of the Congress that it allowed the mistakes of leaders pass away freely and unnoticed and made vivisection easy by their policy. The fear about such Press—weak and subservient as it was—could not therefore dislodge me from my resolve.

120. It is stated in some quarters that the people could not have got the independence unless Pakistan was conceded. But I took it to be an utterly incorrect and untrue

view. To me it appears to be merely a poor excuse to justify the action taken by the leaders. The leaders of the Gandhian creed often claim to have conquered 'Swarajya' by their struggle. If they had conquered Swarajya, then it would be clearly seen that it is most ridiculous to say that those Britishers who yielded, were in a position to lay down the condition of Pakistan before the grant of independence could be effective. To my mind there could be only one reason for Gandhiji and his followers to give their consent to the creation of Pakistan and it is that these people were accustomed to make a show of hesitation and resistance in the beginning and ultimately to surrender to the Muslim demands.

121. Pakistan was conceded on the 15th of August 1947, and how? Pakistan was conceded by deceiving the people and without any consideration for the feelings and opinions of the people- of Punjab, Bengal, N.W.F. Province, Sind, etc. Indivisible Bharat was divided into two and in one of its parts a theocratic State was established. The Muslims obtained the fruit of their anti-national movements and actions in the shape of Pakistan. The leaders of the Gandhian creed ridiculed the opponents of Pakistan as traitors and communal minded, while they themselves helped in the establishment of a Muslim State in India yielding to the demands of Mr. Jinnah. This event of Pakistan had upset the tranquility of my mind. But even after the establishment of Pakistan if this Gandhian Government had taken any steps to protect the interests of Hindus in Pakistan it could have been possible for me to control my mind which was terribly shaken on account of this terrible deception of the people. But, after handing over crores of Hindus to the mercy of the Muslims of Pakistan, Gandhiji and his followers have been advising them not to leave Pakistan but continue to stay on. The

Hindus thus were caught in the hands of Muslim authorities quite unaware and in such circumstances series of calamities followed one after the other. When I bring to my mind all these happenings my body simply feels a horror of burning fire, even now.

122. Every day that dawned, brought forth the news about thousands of Hindus being massacred, Sikhs numbering 15,000 having been shot dead, hundreds of women torn of their clothes being made naked and taken into procession and that Hindu women were being sold in the market places like cattle. Thousands and thousands of Hindus had to run away for their lives and they had lost everything of theirs. A long line of refugees extending over the length of 40 miles was moving towards the Indian Union. How was this terrible happening being counter-acted by the Union Government? Oh, by throwing bread to the refugees from the air!

123. These atrocities and the blood-bath would have, to some extent been checked if the Indian Government had lodged strong protests against the treatment meted out to the Minorities in Pakistan or even if a cold threat had been held out, the Muslims in India being treated in the same manner as a measure of retaliation. But the Government which was under the thumb of Gandhiji resorted to absolutely different ways. If the grievances of the minorities in Pakistan were voiced in the Press, it was dubbed as an attempt to spread disaffection amongst the communities and made an offence and the Congress Government in several Provinces started demanding securities under the Press Emergency Powers Act, one after the other. I was alone served with notices demanding securities to the extent of Rs. 16,000/- and in the Bombay Province alone nearly 900 such cases have occurred, as is stated by the Home Member, Mr. Morarjibhai Desai in

this Court. Nothing was done to redress the grievances of the Press even though Press deputations waited upon the Ministers. Thus there was total disappointment in my attempt to bring pressure by peaceful means upon the Congress Governments guided by Gandhian creed.

124. When all these happenings were taking place in Pakistan, Gandhiji did not even by a single word protest and censure to the Pakistan Government or the Muslims concerned. The Muslim atrocities resorted to in Pakistan to root out the Hindu culture and the Hindu society, have been entirely due to the teachings of Gandhiji and his behaviour. If the Indian politics had been handled in a practical manner there would never have been the terrible human slaughter as has taken place—a thing without any precedent in History.

125. The most noticeable and important thing is that Gandhiji never cared for the opinion of the people so far as Muslims were concerned. His theme of non-violence had now been deeply soaked in human blood and it was impossible for people to entertain any idea in favour of Pakistan. So long as there is a theocratic State and Government by the side of Indian Union, the peace and tranquility of the Union shall ever remain in danger. But in spite of all these facts, Gandhiji had taken in his hand the task of a propaganda which even in the staunchest adherent of the Muslim League would scarcely have been able to do for stopping the spread of unfavourable opinion about Pakistan in the minds of the people.

126. About this very time he resorted to his last fast unto death. Every condition given by him for giving up the fast was in favour of Muslims and against the Hindus.

127. One of the seven conditions imposed by Gandhiji for the breaking of his fast unto death related to the

mosques in Delhi occupied by the refugees. This condition was to the effect that all the mosques in Delhi which were occupied by the refugees should be vacated or got vacated and be made over to the Muslims. Gandhiji got this condition accepted by the Government and a number of leaders by sheer coercion brought to bear upon them by his fast. On that day I happened to be in Delhi and I have personally seen some of the events that have occurred in getting this condition carried out to its full. Those were the days of bitter or extreme cold and on the day Gandhiji broke his fast it was also raining. Owing to this unusual weather condition, the pricking atmosphere made even person in well-placed position shiver. Families after families of refugees who had come to Delhi for shelter were driven out and while doing so no provision was made for their shelter and stay. One or two families taking with them their children, women-folk and what little belongings they had with them and saying: *'Gandhiji, do give us a place for shelter'* even approached to Birla House. Was it ever possible for the cries of these poor Hindu people to reach Gandhiji living in the palatial Birla House? I witnessed with my own eyes this scene which would have melted the heart of even a hard-hearted person. But thoughts even deeper than this began to come to my mind. Was it out of fun that the refugees found these mosques to be better than their own houses from which they were ousted? Was not Gandhiji aware of the reasons and circumstances that compelled the refugees to occupy the mosques? No Temple and no Gurudwara exists in the part of the country that has become Pakistan. These refugees had seen with their own eyes, their temples and Gurudwaras being desecrated by filthy use made of them simply for the purpose of insulting the Sikhs and Hindus. The refuges had come—fled to Delhi having had to leave everything belonging to them and there was no place of shelter for them in Delhi. What wonderful thing there could be if the refugees brought to their minds again and again their own hearths and homes in the Punjab and N.W.F. Province while they were either taking shelter at the sides of the streets or under a tree some how? It was under such circumstances that these refugees had resorted to and occupied the mosques? They were living under the roof in mosques and in doing so, were not these mosques being used for the benefit of humanity? While Gandhiji created the conditions of evacuating the refugees from the mosques occupied by them; had he also asked the Government and the people concerned, to provide some alternative arrangement for their shelter, before getting the mosques evacuated. It would have shown some human touch in his demand. While Gandhiji made a demand for the evacuation of the mosques by the refugees; had he also demanded that the temples in Pakistan should be handed over to the Hindus by the Muslims, or some other similar condition. That would have shown. That Gandhiji's teaching of non-violence, his anxiety for Hindu-Muslim unity and his belief in soul force had been taken or understood as being impartial, spirited and non-communal. Gandhiji was shrewd enough to know that while undertaking a fast unto death, had he imposed such condition on the Muslims in Pakistan, there would have hardly been any Muslim found who could have shown some grief if the fast ended in the death of Gandhiji. It was for this reason that he purposely avoided imposing any condition on the Muslims. It was clearly in his past experience that Mr. Jinnah was not at all perturbed or influenced by his fast and that the Muslim League hardly attached any value to the 'Inner Voice' of Gandhiji.

128. It would not be out of place to state here that the remains (ashes) of Gandhiji were distributed in large towns and many rivers in India and abroad but the said ashes could not be immersed in the Holy Indus passing through the Pakistan in spite of the endeavours of Shri Shree Prakash, the Indian High Commissioner in Pakistan.

129. Let us then take the case of 55 crores. Here, I read from the Indian Information dated 2nd February 1948 the following extracts:

1. Extracts from the speech of the Honourable Sardar Vallabhai Patel at the press conference held on 12th January, 1948.
2. Extract from the speech of the Honourable Sir Shanmukham Chetty.
3. India's spontaneous gesture of goodwill, and
4. An extract from the Honourable Prime Minister's statement.

Gandhiji himself has said about these 55 crores that it is always very difficult to make any Government to alter its decision. But the Government have altered and changed their original decision of withholding the payment of Rs. 55 crores to Pakistan and the reason for doing so was the fast unto death, (Gandhiji's sermon at Prayer-Meeting held on or about the 21st of January 1948). The decision to with-hold the payment of Rs. 55 crores to Pakistan was taken up by our Government which claims to be the people's Government. But this decision of the people's Government was reversed to suit the tune of Gandhiji's fast. It was evident to me that the force of public opinion was nothing but a trifle when compared with the leanings of Gandhiji favouring to Pakistan.

130. The creation of Pakistan is the result of the Muslim hostility to the national movement of India. A

number of people who showed their allegiance to Pakistan have been clapped in jail as fifth columnists by this very Government. But to my mind Gandhiji himself was the greatest supporter and advocate of Pakistan and no power could have any control on him in this attitude of his.

131. In these circumstances the only effective remedy to relieve the Hindus from the Muslim atrocities was, to my mind, to remove Gandhiji from this world.

132. Gandhiji is being referred as the Father of the Nation—an epithet of high reverence. If so, he has failed in his paternal duty in as much as he has acted very treacherously to the nation by his consenting to the partitioning of it. Had Gandhiji really maintained his opposition to the creation of Pakistan, the Muslim League could have had no strength to claim it and the Britishers also could not have created it in spite of all their utmost efforts for its establishment. The reason for this is not far to seek. The people of this country were eager and vehement in their opposition to Pakistan. But Gandhiji played false with the people and gave parts of the country to the Muslims for the creation of Pakistan. I stoutly maintain that Gandhiji in doing so has failed in his duty which was incumbent upon him to carry out, as the Father of the Nation. He has proved to be the Father of Pakistan. It was for this reason alone that I as a dutiful son of Mother India thought it my duty to put an end to the life of the so-called Father of the Nation, who had played a very prominent part in bringing about the vivisection of the country—Our Motherland.

133. The case of Hyderabad has also the same history, it is not at all necessary to refer to the trocious misdeeds perpetrated by the Nizam's Ministers and the Razakars. Laik Ali the Prime Minister of Hyderabad had an interview

with Gandhiji during the last week of January 1948. It was evident from the manner in which Gandhiji looked at these Hyderabad affairs, that Gandhiji would soon start his experiments of non-violence in the State of Hyderabad and treat Kasim Razvi as his adopted son just as Suhrawardy. It was not at all difficult to see that it was impossible for the Government in spite of all the powers to take any strong measures against the Muslim State like Hyderabad so long as Gandhiji was there. Had the Government then decided to take any military or police action against Hyderabad it would have been compelled to withdraw its decision just as it was done in the case of the payment of Rs. 55 crores in the name of Hindu-Muslim unity, for Gandhiji would have gone on fast unto death and Government's hands would have been tied to save the life of Gandhiji.

134. The practice of non-violence according to Gandhiji is to endure or put up with the blows of the aggressor without showing any resistance either by weapon or by physical force, Gandhiji has, while describing his non-violence given the example of a 'tiger becoming a follower of the creed of non-violence after the cows allowed themselves to be killed and swallowed in such large numbers that the tiger ultimately got tired of killing them.' It will be remembered that at Kanpur, Ganesh Shanker Vidyarthi fell a victim to the murderous assault by the Muslims of the place on him. Gandhiji has often cited this submission to the Muslims' blows as an ideal example of embracing death for the creed of nonviolence I firmly believed and believe that the nonviolence of the type described above will lead the nation to ruin and make it easy for Pakistan to enter the remaining India and occupy the same.

135. Briefly speaking, I thought over and foresaw that I shall be totally ruined and the only thing that I could expect from the people would be nothing but hatred and that I shall have lost all my honour even more valuable than my life, if I were to kill Gandhiji. But at the same time I felt that the Indian politics in the absence of Gandhiji would surely be practical, able to retaliate, and would be powerful with armed forces. No doubt my own future would be totally ruined but the nation would be saved from the inroads of Pakistan. People may even call and dub me as devoid of any sense or foolish, but the nation would be free to follow the course founded on reason which I consider to be necessary for sound nation building. After having fully considered the question, I took the final decision in the matter but I did not speak about it to any one whatsoever. I took courage in my both hands and I did fire the shots at Gandhiji on 30th January, 1948 on the prayer grounds in Birla House.

136. There now remains hardly anything for me to say. If devotion to one's country amounts to a sin, I admit I have committed that sin. If it is meritorious, I humbly claim the merit thereof. I fully and confidently believe that if there be any other court of justice beyond the one founded by the mortals, my act will not be taken as unjust. If after the death there be no such place to reach or to go, there is nothing to be said. I have resorted to the action I did purely for the benefit of the humanity. I do say that my shots were fired at the person whose policy and action had brought wrack and ruin and destruction to lakhs of Hindus.

137. Really speaking, my life also came to an end simultaneously with the shots fired by me at Gandhiji. Since then I have been passing my days as if in trance and meditation. Whatever I have seen and observed during this time has given me complete satisfaction.

138. The problem of the State of Hyderabad which had been unnecessarily delayed and postponed has been rightly solved by our Government by the use of armed force after the demise of Gandhiji. The present Government of the remaining India is seen taking the course of practical politics. The Home Member is said to have expressed the view that the nation must be possessed of armies fully equipped with modern arms and fighting machinery. While giving out such expressions he does say that such a step would be in keeping with the ideals of Gandhiji. He may say so for his satisfaction. But one must not forget that if that were so there would be no difference in the means for the protection of the country devised by Hitler, Mussolini or Churchill or Roosevelt and the scheme based on non-violence as envisaged by Gandhiji. It would then be impossible to say that there was any new and special message of non-violence of Gandhiji.

139. I am prepared to concede that Gandhiji did undergo sufferings for the sake of the nation. He did bring about an awakening in the minds of the people. He also did nothing for personal gain, but it pains me to say that he was not honest enough to acknowledge the defeat and failure of the principle of non-violence on all sides. I have read the lives of other intelligent and powerful Indian patriots who have made sacrifices even greater than those done by Gandhiji. I have even seen personally some of them. But whatever that may be, I shall bow in respect of the service done by Gandhiji to the country, and to Gandhiji himself for the said service and before I fired the shots I actually wished him and bowed to him in reverence. But I do maintain that even this servant of the country had no right to vivisect the country—the image of our worship—by deceiving the people. But he did it all the same. There was no legal machinery by which such an offender could

be brought to book and it was therefore that I resorted to the firing of shots at Gandhiji as that was the only thing for me to do.

140. Had this act not been done by me, of course it would have been better for me. But circumstances were beyond my control. So strong was the impulse of my mind that I felt that this man should not be allowed to meet a natural death so that the world may know that he had to pay the penalty of his life for his unjust, anti-national and dangerous favouritism towards a fanatical section of the country. I decided to put an end to this matter and to the further massacre of lacs of Hindus for no fault of theirs. May God now pardon him for his egoistic nature which proved to be too disastrous for the beloved sons of this Holy Land.

141. I bear no ill-will or enmity towards any individual. Nor do I think that any person is inimical towards me personally. I do say that I had no respect for the present Government owing to their policy which was unfairly favourable to the Muslims. At the same time I could clearly see that the policy was entirely due to the presence of Gandhiji. In the absence of such pressure the way is now open for the establishment of a Secular State in the true sense of that word. I have to say with great regret that the hon'ble Prime Minister Pandit Nehruji quite forgets that his actions and deeds are at times opposed to each other, when he talks about secular State in season and out of season; because it is significant to note that the hon'ble Pandit Nehruji has himself taken a leading part in acquiescing to the establishment of Pakistan, a theocratic State. But he should have realised that it will never bring prosperity to Indian Union with a State founded on fanatically blind religious faith and basis by its side. After having considered absolutely to myself,

my mind impelled me to take the action against Gandhiji. No one has brought and could bring any pressure on me in this act of mine.

142. The Honourable Court may take any view in regard to the impulse my mind received and the action I did thereunder and may pass against me such orders of sentence as may be proper. I have no desire to say anything about it. I do not desire any mercy to be shown to me. I do not also wish that anyone on my behalf should beg for mercy towards me.

143. Several persons are arrayed along with me in this trial as conspirators. I have already said that in the act I did, I had no companions and I alone am solely responsible for my act. Had they not been arraigned with me I would not have even given any defence for me as would be clear from the fact that I desired and enjoined upon my counsel not to cross-examine any of the witnesses connected with the incident of the 30th of January, 1948.

144. I have already made it clear that personally I had never accepted the idea of peaceful demonstration even on 20th January, 1948 even for effective propaganda. However, I agreed to join this peaceful demonstration in the prayer-meeting of Gandhiji, though with great reluctance. But as luck would have it, I could not take part in it. And when I found that even such demonstration could not be effectively staged for one reason or the other, I became rather disappointed and desperate. Efforts of Mr. Apte and others to secure volunteer made at Bombay, Poona and Gwalior bore no fruit. I could not then see any other way except to take the extreme course.

145. With these thoughts in mind, while moving through the refugee Camp in Delhi, I met a photographer with a camera on his back. He asked me to get myself

photographed. He seemed to be a refugee. I agreed and got myself photographed by him. On returning to the Delhi Railway Station, I wrote two letters to Apte giving a faint idea of my mental state enclosing therewith my photographs as I felt it my duty to inform Mr. Nanarao Apte as he was my close associate in my business of the press; one of such letter was addressed to him personally at his home address at Poona and another was sent to the Hindu Rashtra Office.

146. I wish to further state that all the statements made by me herein are entirely true and correct and each of them is made by reference to authoritative reference books. I have made use of the several issues of the Indian Information, an official organ of the Government of India for the information of the public, Indian Year Book, History of the Congress, Gandhiji's Autobiography, Congress Bulletins issued from time to time and the files of Harijan and Young India, and Gandhiji's post prayer speeches. I have made this rather long statement not because I want the people to eulogise my act. My only object in doing so is to leave no room for any misunderstanding about me, and there should be no vagueness in their mind about my views.

147. May the country properly known as Hindustan be again united and be one and may the people be taught to discard the defeatist mentality leading them to submit to the aggressors. This is my last wish and prayer to the Almighty.

148. I have now finished, but before I sit down must sincerely and respectfully express my gratitude to Your Honour for the patient hearing given, courtesy shown and facilities given to me. Similarly I express my gratitude to my legal advisers and counsel for their legal help in this

great trial. I have no ill-will towards the Police Officers connected with this case. I sincerely thank them for the kindness and the treatment given by them to me. Similarly, I also thank the Jail authorities for the good treatment given by them.

149. It is a fact that in the presence of a crowd numbering 300 to 400 people I did fire shots at Gandhiji in open daylight. I did not make any attempt to run away. In fact, I never entertained any-idea of running away. I did not try to shoot myself it was never my intention to do so, for, it was my ardent desire to give vent to my thoughts in an open Court.

150. My confidence about the moral side of my action has not been shaken even by the criticism levelled against it on all sides. I have no doubt honest writers of history will weigh my act and find the true value thereof on some day in future.

AKHANDA BHARAT AMAR RAHE
VANDE MATARAM

Sd/-Atma Charan
8th November 1948
(Special Judge)

(Nathuram V. Godse)
Delhi, 8.11.1948

The Arguments Before the Special Judge
Judgment and Appeals to the High Court

The statements of the accused, which were recorded from the 8th of November 1948 to 22nd of November 1948, ran into 260 pages. The defence had also put up 119 documents.

Out of the other accused, Madan Lal Pahwa had confessed that he had ignited the gun-cotton slab at the prayer meeting compound on the 20th January 1948 when Gandhiji's post prayer lecture was going on. His action was only to record his protest against the pro-Muslim policy of Gandhiji which was against the national interests, and that there was neither any conspiracy nor was he a member of it.

Digamber Badge having turned an approver, his statement was bound to favour the prosecution story.

Nathuram Godse had unequivocally stated that it was he who deliberately fired the pistol with intent to kill and gave his elaborate reasons for doing so. He had denied the charge of conspiracy. All the other accused had denied the charge of conspiracy, or their alleged participation in it.

The arguments of the Prosecution and the Defence commenced on 1.12.1948 and continued day to day. Nathuram V. Godse argued his own case, while Shri P.R. Das of Patna argued the case on behalf of Veer Savarkar. Two happenings in the Court-room cannot be omitted from mentioning.

At the trial, Nathuram had said that two bullets had passed from the pistol, while the medical report had found three. Shri C.K. Daphtary submitted that this argument of 'two bullets' was being put forward by the accused

(Nathuram) in order to make ground for 'benefit of doubt'. Nathuram promptly stood up and replied;

> The pistol was automatic. The trigger was pressed once. Whether two bullets passed or three, is immaterial, for even one was sufficient, and that one was fired by me. If on this discrepancy, any 'benefit of doubt' accrues, the same may be granted to the prosecution.

The other one was when Shri C.K. Daphtary in midst of his argument referred to the incident of the assassination as an 'immoral' act. Nathuram stood up and took a strong exception to it.

> At least as far as this case is concerned the Prosecution has no right to discuss the morality of the act, nor does the Court, I humbly submit, have any jurisdiction to decide that issue. The concepts of morality would be seen to be changing from society to society, from country to country and from century to century. In a particular society it would be considered immoral for women not to use the veil (parda), while in others it may be perfectly moral. In some countries drinking liquors would not be considered immoral at all. In a certain century teaching Vedic lore to the non-Brahmins might have been looked upon as highly immoral, but today it is not. Such is the way concepts of morality go on changing. Nobody, therefore, will be able to determine any standard norm for judging morality or immorality for all times, irrespective of country or climate.
>
> If the Prosecution wants to maintain that killing is absolutely, wholly and without any exception, 'immoral', then it will have to be admitted that the

present rulers themselves are behaving most immorally, because occasionally they have to resort to firing bullets on people.

The Prosecution has neither the legal nor the moral right to bring forth this question. If the attorneys on the Government side are paid a little more than what they actually receive now they would unhesitatingly work as defence counsels. Can it, therefore, be said only on that count that they have abandoned morality or the moral side?

The Court only has jurisdiction to decide the legality or otherwise of my action but in so far as morality is concerned, it is, a matter of my conviction that what I did was wholly moral and upon those convictions, this Court has no jurisdiction.

Arguments were concluded on 30.12.1948. We had been given the impression that the judgment would be delivered after a month.

The 10th of February 1949 dawned. All the accussed reached the Court. As the Judge Shri Atmacharan of the Special Court, Red Fort, went on pronouncing the sentences on the accused one after another, the suspense in their minds came to an end, and they could compose themselves ably.

Nathuram and Nana Apte were sentenced 'to be hanged by the neck till they are dead' while Vishnu Karkare, Madan Lal Pahava, (Gopal Godse), Shankar Kistaiyya, and Dr. Parchure were sentenced to 'transportation for life'. Digambar Badge was tendered a pardon as he had turned an approver, while Veer Savarkar was honourably acquitted. There was an uneasy calm after the pronouncement of the judgment, and then we all convicts shouted with one voice:

Swatantrya Lakshmi Id Jai, Victory to Hindu Nation; Long live undivided India! Vande Mataram.

The day of sentence seemed to have passed away quickly, because of its newness and because of the quick succession of events that took place that day. When got up the next morning all realised that they had passed into an altogether new world. 'sleep of all the accussed was constantly disturbed because of the fetters. Howsoever despicable our condition might have been, all of them derived happiness from the thought that at least there was no one of the acquaintance to see them in that state.

A period of fifteen days was allowed to prefer appeals against the verdict of the Special Court. Our Lawyers were busy with the filing the appeals. So they paid a visit within two or three days, but no one from amongst accused had any trace of sorrow or misery on their faces. Nathuram did not appeal against the charge proved under Section 302 of the Penal Code and the sentence passed under it. His appeal was against the other charges taken to be established. All were removed to Ambala Central Jail in a Police van via Panipat after two months.

Nathuram and Nana were taken to the condemned cells. The remaining five were sent to a yard. They could go to the death—cells and see Nathuram and Nana Apte quite often. The sympathetic attitude of the—officers in the Ambala prison was the greatest satisfaction. It was perhaps prompted by two causes.

These authorities observed them very closely for some days. They found no trace of criminal tendencies in any of them. Secondly, they knew in their heart of hearts the reason why Gandhiji was assassinated.

Accused received the books of the printed records of the Mahatma Gandhi Murder Case on the 14th April 1949 and the day for hearing appeals was just fifteen days thereafter. Nathuram forthwith started studying these books and jotting down notes.

The question whether Nathuram Godse should be allowed to argue in person or be forced to accept a pleader provided by the Government as 'his pleader', also attracted a judicial adjudication and this one was given on 24.3.1949 and is reported as *Nathuram V. Godse vs The Crown.* (AIR 1949 East Punjab 321). The Court accepted his request and allowed Nathuram Godse to appear in person and argue his case. He was taken to Simla.

Nathuram's 40th birthday was on 19th of May 1949 while he was at Simla. His younger brother Dattatraya, who was released from detention from the Yeravada Central Prison (Pune, Maharashtra) a few months earlier, had gone to Simla to attend the Court for hearing the proceedings.

In the evening of the 19th May, he was preparing to go to see Nathuram to greet him on the occasion of his birthday, when a girl came to see him. Dattatraya had casually seen her in the Court.

The girl requested Dattatraya to take her to Nathuram as she wanted to see him. 'But', Dattatraya told her 'only relatives are permitted'. She replied: 'I shall manage that. Simply take me to the cell where he is lodged.'

She then disclosed her identity. She was the daughter of a sitting High Court judge but not on the Bench which was hearing the appeals. She had a small basket of fruit and some flowers. The authorities noted the name of Dattatraya as the only visitor and allowed the girl to accompany him.

The girl paid her respects to Nathuram, and offered the flowers and fruit to him. In a few words she expressed her appreciation. From the bottom of the basket she took out a sweater. She wanted it to pass on to Nathuram. The officer on duty checked it and allowed.

'Wear this sweater one day while arguing the case. I shall feel happy.' She said. Nathuram thanked her and agreed to wear it.

The late Maulana Azad has observed in his book, 'India Wins Freedom' on page 225, 'Some women from respectable families sent him (Nathuram) a sweater they had knitted for him', whereby he wanted to show how even the elite classes also considered Nathuram a hero. It was a fact. It was by way of hero-worship.

The Full Bench of the East Punjab High Court comprising of Justices Amarnath Bhandari, Achhru Ram and Gopaldas Khosla, started the final hearing of appeals on the 23rd of May 1949. The hearing continued day to day for a fortnight.

About Nathuram's stay at Simla a special mention has to be made of the curiosity that it had aroused amongst the people because he himself was to conduct his own case and that too with the sword of Death hanging constantly over his head. It was public knowledge that he had not appealed against the death sentence passed on him by the Special Court in the Red Fort. People wondered how Nathuram could ever attain that equanimity of mind to argue his case in a coherent manner. The audience mainly consisted of the high-brow people who formed a major section of the then population of Simla.

Justice Shri Khosla [who was on the Bench of the East Punjab High Court], in his book, 'The Murder of the Mahatma', had this to say :

> The highlight of the appeal before us was the discourse delivered by Nathuram Godse in his

defence. He spoke for several hours discussing, in the first instance, the facts of the case and then the motive which had prompted him to take Mahatma Gandhi's life.

The audience was visibly and audibly moved. There was a deep silence when he ceased speaking. Many women were in tears and men were coughing and searching for their handkerchiefs. This silence was accentuated and made deeper by the sound of an occasional subdued sniff or a muffled cough.

I have however no doubt that had the audience of that day been constituted into a jury and entrusted with the task of deciding Godse's appeal, they would have, brought in a verdict of 'not guilty' by an overwhelming majority.

The High Court judgment was delivered on the 22nd of June 1949. Dr. Parchure and Shankar Kistaiyya were acquitted. The conviction of all others including the death sentences on Nathuram Godse and Nana Apte were maintained.

The Events After the High Court Judgment, and till Execution of the Death Sentence.

After the hearing of the appeals was over, Nathuram was brought back to Ambala Central jail and lodged in the condemned cell yard in the middle of June 1949. Nana Apte was already there. They both remained there till the end.

While at Simla in the temporary custody made for Nathuram, he received a letter which was duly censored by the authorities and passed on to him. It was from **Shri Ramdas Gandhi** one of the sons of Gandhiji. The lettter reads:

Khalasi Line, Nagpur, C.P.
Dated 17th May, 1949.

Dear Nathuram Godse,

The writer of this letter is the son of one you seem to take great pride in having assassinated.

I am sure, you will one day realise that you have only put an end to my father's perishable body and nothing more. Because not only in my case but in the case of millions all over the world, the spirit of my father still rules their hearts. This stands proved by the homage that has been paid to my father by nations and people all over the world.

You know that today everyone all over the world is thirsting and pining for peace. But you must have stood aghast to find that amongst the biggest war-lords of the present age to say and believe that it is not the atomic energy that is going to bring peace to the world, but it is the mutual understanding and respect for one by the other—better understood by the millions of this country by the simple and significant words 'Satya and Ahimsa'.

I hope that the above facts will help in the dissolution of the mist of misunderstanding your mind and vision seem to be shrouded with, once you rid your mind of .this misunderstanding. I have no doubt, you will repent and realise that what you have done is a deed never to be repeated but shunned for all the times, be it in the interest of one's own religion or political creed or anything else. You are reported to have stated very recently that you are a man of 'reason and logic.' I, therefore, urge upon you to ponder over my above heart-pourings and if you do so, you will find that you have not the least served the cause so very dear to you by having done what you have done.

Yours truly,
Sd/- R. Gandhi

P.S. I may inform you that on 1.5.1949, I have addressed a letter to the Governor General of India, giving him my reason why you should not be made to suffer the penalty awarded by the Special Tribunal to look into the charges framed against you by the authorities concerned.

Sd/- R. Gandhi

Nathuram replied:

'OM'

Simla

3rd June, 1949.

Dear Brother Shri Ramdas Gandhi,

Received your most kind letter of the 17th May, 1949, yesterday. As a human being I have no words to express my feelings for the wounds that you and your relatives must have received by the tragic end of your revered father, fey my hands. But at the same time I state that there is the other side to look at. I am not in a position to write all my thoughts on paper nor am I in a position to see you personally. But certainly you are in a position to see me in jail before my execution.

You say that you have heard that 'I am a man of reason and logic'. True. But you will be surprised to note that I am a man of very powerful sentiments also, and 'Devotion' to my mother-land is the topmost of the same.

You say that once my mind is free from misunderstandings then I shall no doubt repent and realise my blunder.

Brother, I say I am an open-minded man always subject to correction. But what is the way to remove my misunderstanding, if any, to make me repent?

Certainly not the gallows, nor 'a big show of mercy, and to commute my punishment. The only way is to see me and to make me realise. Until now I have come across nothing which will make me repent.

I have received Several letters from some prominent Christian Missions and according to their faith and teaching of the 'Holy Bible', they have tried to give me some message. Their stand is quite intelligible. But yours is the first letter that I have received which resembles to some extent to the well known or more known teachings of your revered father. Really this is surprising. I have received many letters full of abuses. I do not consider that they were written by any disciple of your father.

Any way, I must request you to see me and if possible with some prominent disciples of your father, particularly who are not interested in any power politics, and to bring to my notice my most fatal mistake.

Otherwise, I shall always feel that this show of mercy is nothing but an eyewash.

If you actually see me and have a talk with me either sentimentally or on reason, who knows you will be able to change me and make me repent or I may change you and make you realise my stand?

The condition of the talk must be that we must stick to the truth alone.

Again I express my utmost regrets as a human being for your sufferings due to the death of your father by my hands.

Yours sincerely,

Sd/- Nathuram V. Godse.

N.B. If you prefer, then please send a copy of this to H.E. the Governor General of the Dominion of India.

Shri Ram Das Gandhi's another letter to Godse:

Khalasi Lines, Nagpur
Dated 13th June, 1949

Dear Shri Nathuram Godse,

Received your letter dated 3rd June, 1949.

I feel happy to find that you are always willing (lit. free) to accept views. Similarly, the wish expressed by you for talking freely with me and with the close associates of my father on the questions whether the ways and means adopted by you have proved to be useful or are likely to prove useful sometime in future in preserving the integrity of our mother land, or preserving the integrity of our centuries—old Hindu religion which is, like any other current religion, aloof from any kind of differences is encouraging.

Similarly, without giving any promise of holding talks with you on behalf of the Government of India as well as on behalf of myself or those who will accompany me, I am making a request to Pandit Jawaharlal Nehru to grant permission today to Shri Vinoba Bhave, Shri Kishorilal Mashruwala and me for holding talks with you on the above-mentioned subject, because it is your sincere desire that it should be so.

If destiny has ordained that the projected talk should take place, the talk will take place only after 25th June 1949 because you should kindly note that it will not be possible for me to go to Delhi from Nagpur and from there to proceed to the place where you have been kept before 25th June.

I think you should not have stipulated the condition, 'we should speak in consonant with truth', because I think that condition was not only unnecessary in my case but also unnecessary in the case of any close associates of my father.

In the meantime, I want to suggest to you that you should spend all available time at your disposal in self introspection and that too by placing full faith in Almighty. You should pray that 'He alone will bestow his favourable benediction on you', because I feel that such favour alone will help in bringing your mistake to your notice. And it will dawn upon you that Gandhiji ultimately knew it well, how to protect our motherland and particularly Hindu religion from insult or injury. If you do this, I am confident that at the end of the projected meeting between you and me you will be able to recite with us the following verse in the 18th Chapter of Bhagavat Gita, which is a perfect poem in beauty and meaning:

अर्जुन उवाच

नष्टो मोहः स्मृतिर्लब्धा त्वत्प्रसादान्मयाच्युत।
स्थितोऽस्मि गतसन्देहः करिष्ये वचनं तव॥

O, Achyuta, because of your favour my ignorance has disappeared. I have regained normalcy. I am herewith all doubts resolved. I will do what you say.

Yours sincerely
Sd/- R.M. Gandhi

Reply sent by NathuramGodse:

Central Prison,
Ambala,
24th June, 1949.

Dear Shri Ramdas Gandhi,

Received your letter dated the 13th instant on 23rd June and noted down the contents.

I am happy that you responded to my request. You may come at any time convenient to you. You can meet me a day before the execution also. I am not impatient about this meeting. I am feeling a kind of satisfaction also by your intention to meet me. If you do not meet me at all owing to some other difficulties, I will not feel anything about it because in your heart you showed readiness to meet me. The sincerity of your purpose is reflected in this. It is sufficient for me.

However, I request you that you should try to bring about this meeting.

I agree with your statement that I should not have stipulated that 'truth alone should be spoken'. Believe me that while writing that it was not my purpose to hurt you. There were mainly two reasons in my mind behind that writing. I have met many so called votaries of the creed of Truth'. However in actual life they bother the least about that creed. I have seen some people distorting truth on vow in the witness box.

And another reason is that I shall perhaps have to speak some bitter truth in our conversation. At least according to my belief, it will be truth and it will be bitter.

Whatever it may be. I have got this much assurance from your letter that I should not be afraid of speaking fearlessly.

I thank you for having reminded me of the verse 'My ignorance has disappeared'.

I have regained normalcy from the Bhagwat Gita. In my opinion not only these verses in the Gita but the whole of the Gita is an invaluable poem replete with meaning and beauty.

After Arjun had said 'I will do as you say' he had directly translated into practice the words of Lord Krishna, 'Remember me and fight'.

Shri Vinoba Bhave is Maharashtrian by birth. You make an enquiry, if possible, into my general character and behaviour prior to the imprisonment, through him (V. Bhave) or through anybody else. It will be perhaps useful to you to know the background of the individual who committed the cruel unlawful act.

Nothing more at present.

Yours sincerely

Sd/- N.V. Godse

24th June 1949

Apart from the said correspondence which amply displays Nathuram's mental equilibrium, deep conviction and yet open mindedness to receive thoughts. His words were:

> Let the disciples of Gandhi satisfy me that I have acted wrong; I shall declare my repentance without asking for any reward for it and go to the gallows.

On the other hand, if I satisfy them of the justifiability of my act they should be honest enough to admit so openly.

Escape from the gallows is no allurement to me. So in that case too I shall gladly climb the platform of the rope.

That a man of Nathuram's calibre should have been the cause of the death of an important politician like Gandhiji, who, as every body knows, had such an unparalleled sway over the Indian political life for the period of nearly thirty five years prior to his assassination, made it imperative for the people to re-examine his antecedents.

That Nathuram remained steadfast till the end need not, I think, be proved by adducing any more evidence than what has been so far cited. Since the time of assassination of Gandhiji till Nathuram's death on the gallows a great span of twenty-one months and a half or six hundred and fifty-five days had elapsed. Throughout all these days Nathuram's daily routine was most systematically observed. Even his daily religious rituals. He had not become averse to eating or drinking, nor did he suffer from sleeplessness.

On the 11th of November 1949 parents of Nathuram Godse sent him a telegram blessing him, to which Nathuram wrote a consolatory letter. A translated summary whereof is as follows :

Ambala,12.11.1949

My most revered Mother and Father,

I have your photographs with me here which I will worship before I deliver myself up and be united with Brahma.

I have no doubt that you are bound to feel extreme, heart-rending grief at my loss, because of our worldly relation in this life. But I am not writing this letter to give vent to my sorrow or to philosophize on it.

You are the students of the Geeta and have also learnt the Puranas. Lord Krishna had recited this Geeta to enlighten Arjun and the very same Lord Krishna had with his Sudarshan wheel chopped off the head of an Aryan King Shishupal, not on a battle-field but on a sacrificial ground, the Rajsooya Yadnyabhoomi! Who will say that Lord Krishna committed sin in doing so? Giving gifts or donations to the wicked is not considered a virtuous act; it is irreligious. For the sake of one single Seeta being forcibly carried away by Ravana a mighty war had to be fought and for the sake of one Draupadi's insult an epic war in Mahabharata had to be waged. Here in our very country in our very presence hundreds and thousands of Hindu women were being molested, raped and carried away forcibly to be converted to Islam and the perpetrators of these atrocious deeds were being helped in all possible ways. In such circumstances I could not sit silent and watch helplessly all this through fear of losing my life or of incurring public censure and wrath. I am sure the blessings of thousands of young women are behind my back to support me.

I have laid down my life at the feet of my beloved Motherland.

My mind is pure and my feelings are absolutely righteous. To beg for my life as alms by pleading for mercy is something I never liked.

Death did not come to me to demand my life; I myself have gone to Him to offer it.

There are millions of people who will shed their tears at this sacrifice of our lives. They are going to share your sorrow.

Akhand Bharat Amar Rahe!
Vande Mataram.

Nathuram continued to read and write regularly till the end. Just on the previous day of the execution he had completed a long letter written to Shri G.T. Madkholkar besides some others and had also signed in the autograph-books of some of the visitors who had obtained permission from the authorities.

The actual process of execution is not the really horrifying thing in a sentence of death; death comes to the condemned convict without any agonies worth speaking of. The greatest horror lies for the convict in passing moment after dreadful moment in absolute loneliness waiting all the time for the executioner's rope.

As a matter of fact the sentence of death is not the sentence of imprisonment but only in a technical sense. Because of the inevitability of the law the condemned convict has necessarily to languish in imprisonment, which is much harder to bear than any other kind of imprisonment.

Nathuram and Nana Apte were not exempted from any rules enforced on condemned convicts.

Even under such depressing and oppressive conditions in the prison the condemned person goes on living, willy-nilly. The person to be executed entertains some hope that perhaps his punishment of death on the gallows may be changed to some other lesser type of punishment or may be quashed altogether and he may be set free, who knows?

So he, beguiled by such a fond hope puts up with all the harassment and vexation of the prison.

Nathuram, however, had never entertained any such hope, because he had not appealed against the sentence of death passed on him and the High Court had no reason to reconsider his conviction on that count. Nana Apte was nonetheless courageous nor less patient.

While all the accused were kept in the special prison in the Red Fort as under trial prisoners, Nathuram, Nana Apte and Savarkar used to have discussions on the Patanjali's Yogasutras.

In their contemporary friends' circle Nana is known as one given to luxurious living while Nathuram is considered to be an ascetic—of course in a little bit exaggerated way of speech.

Nathuram and Apte continued to be lodged in the condemned cells of the Ambala Central Jail. Roughly a week before the execution Central Government Home Ministry declared the date of execution of Nathuram and Apte as 15th of November 1949. Relatives were telegraphically informed to see the condemned convicts for the last time on 14 November 1949. The relatives numbering about 30 to 35 had gathered to have the last 'Darshan' of both Nathuram and Apte.

The meeting was gloomy in the beginning on part of the visitors, but was very pleasant in the end. Enquired one of the relatives:

> Well Nathuram it is the custom to immerse the ashes (remains) in Ganga at Haridwar, or Triveni Sangam (meeting of three rivers) at Prayagraj or Godavari at Nasik. How come, that you chose 'Sindhu' river for the immersion of your remains?

The reply was prompt:

That is the only river which has remained unpolluted.

There was a huge laughter. All those present had known that Gandhiji's remains could not be sunk in the 'Sindhu'. Nathuram had even made a reference of it at para 128 of his statement. The relatives had also known about the Will of Nathuram. His answer was thus bound to evoke laughter. The conversation was in Marathi. The jailor who was a refugee from Punjab, asked to know what the wit was. He was told of the answer in Hindi and he too could not miss laughing.

The meeting of Nana Apte and his wife, Champutai, was extremely touching. 'Look', Nana said to her, 'from tomorrow onwards you have to weep, weep and weep! These few moments have come to our lot to afford us a hearty talk in privacy. Why not spend them cheerfully?'

The group returned very joyously seeing both of the condemned persons beyond the reach of fear, even at the threshold of the Death. They were to be hanged the next morning.

Karkare, Madan Lal and Gopal, went to see Nathuram and Nana once again. They recited some chapters from the Bhagwat Geeta, particularly the II, the XI and the XVIII, which Nathuram liked most.

The jailors on duty talked and talked and talked with them all the night, saying that they would not have any opportunity thereafter. It was true. The Superintendent, the jailors and the staff also developed affection towards them because of the moral foundation behind the act and high morale of the condemned convicts.

In the tender rays of the morning sun at 8 o'clock both Nathuram and Nana were ready to face the gallows with the map of the Undivided India, the saffron-colour flag and a copy of the Bhagwat Geeta in their hands. Apte was delighted to see the gentle sunlight and at once exclaimed with joy, *'Pandit, how charming, how bewitching is this early morning Sunlight!'*

'Oh dear,' responded Nathuram equally enthusiastically, *'it's almost always so very pleasant in Simla.'*

'Akhand Bharat Amar Rahe!' (Long live the Undivided India!) and *Vande Mataram* (Bow I here to Thee, O Mother!) were the skyrending slogans on their lips when they both entered the execution enclosure. Once inside the enclosure, and with the ropes round their necks, they both sang at the top of their voices:

Namaste Soda Vatsale Matribhume
Twaya Hindubhume Sukham Vardhitoham
Mahanmangale Punyabhume Twadarthe
Patatwesh Kayo Namaste, Namaste!'
Vande Mataram

Translated into English it meant:

Bow to Thee, O, Living Motherland, forever!
Brought up by Thee am I in happiness,
O, Land of the Hindus!
O, most sacred and holy Land, for Thy sake
May this body fall! Bow to Thee, Bow to Thee,
for ever and ever!

VandeMataram

No sooner had these words mingled with the atmosphere than the hangman pulled the rod of the planks from under their feet and the two lives were blended for ever with the Five Elements! The timing of the hangman's move It would described as an act of nature,—for so perfectly timed it was that the planks moved after the word *'Vande'* leaving just enough time for *'Mataram'* to be uttered before the rope took over.

The cremation was inside the jail premises. On the following day of the execution of Nathuram and Apte, when these visitors came back to the Ambala Railway Station for their return journey, the station was overcrowded with the local people for bidding adieu to them and the whole station yard resounded with the loud shouts of '...... ki jai, as a mark of sympathy.

Nathuram made his 'Will', in which he had expressed his last wish which enjoined upon 'the people' to let his ashes fall into the Indus,—the Sindhu, and that too only when that river would come under the Indian National Flag as an indivisible, integral part of the Indian Nation : may it then be after a lapse of many years and after as many generations! A copy of his Will appears in the appendix.

That was the end of Nathuram V. Godse and Nana Apte accused 1 & 2. The other accused served their jail terms; whereafter they were set free.

Profile of Nathuram Godse and of the other Accused

1. **Nathuram Vinayak Godse,** *(Accused No. 1)* was born on 19th of May 1910 at Baramati district Poona. He hailed from Chitpavan Brahmin community. Nathuram's grandfather was an erudite Brahmin, named Vamanrao. Besides agriculture he carried on the profession of priesthood. His native village was Uksan.

Vamanrao had three daughters and one son, who was named Vinayak, born in 1875. When Vinayak, in the final year of his school education, was seventeen year old, he was married to Godavari, aged about 10. Her name was changed to Lakshmi after marriage.

When he passed his school-leaving examination, he was employed in the Postal Department, on a monthly salary of five rupees for the first three months and then fifteen rupees. Lakshmi gave birth to a son. It was the 19th of May 1910. He was nicknamed 'Nathu'. This nickname was later on routinised as Nathuram.

Nathuram began his primary education at Baramati. His thread-ceremony was performed in the Ram Mandir. Nathuram had committed to memory a great deal from the 'Selections from the Medieval and Nineteen Century Marathi Poetry, 'Navaneeta'.

Nathuram took to reading at an early age. He began reading the 'Kesari' not because he understood its contents, but simply for the love of reading. Naturally whatever was published on the subject of the attainment of independence influenced him first indirectly and later directly.

After he passed the fourth standard in the Primary School he was kept with his aunt in Pune for his English education. Nathuram's mode of reasoning was thoroughly logical which got reflected when he had grown up. In his childhood he was more sentimental than rational.

In every generation there are always some young enthusiasts who take keen interest in social work and Nathuram was one of them.

While at Lonavla, a child fell into a well and his mother and other women around raised a hue and cry. At that time Nathuram and one of his friends were passing by the well. The well had steps. The child was not drowned. So Nathuram immediately jumped into the well, took up the child and climbed the steps up.

The child saved was a Mahar by caste, said by some was an untouchable. Whatever might have been the reasons, which led him to join whole-heartedly the campaign against casteism, this must have been one of them.

Nathuram was, however, consciously watchful of the active politics of the day. The result of this political consciousness in him was that his attention was diverted from his studies. As the Satyagraha movement was gathering momentum at that time under the leadership of Gandhiji, he asked his father if he could join it. The father told him that education must have precedence over everything else.

Nathuram, studying in the Nootan Marathi Vidyalaya, appeared for his Matriculation Examination. In the meanwhile the father was transferred to Ratnagiri, during the year 1929-30. This transfer proved to be a revolutionary event not only in the life of Vinayakrao but in that of Nathuram also.

Veer Savarkar was living then at Ratnagiri. He was under government restriction and was forbidden to leave the precincts of Ratnagiri district and from writing, discussing or lecturing on political issues. Savarkar was then known to the people only surreptitiously. His series of articles named Mazi Janamthep' (My Transportation for Life) was by then published in book form. It was later banned and confiscated. Nathuram had come to know the greatness of Veer Savarkar.

Off and on Nathuram could hear from the very lips of Veer Savarkar his exploits in London. Once he brought home a copy of Savarkar's 'War of Independence of 1857', which he used to read it at night. Nathuram gladly undertook the work of copying the writing of Veer Savarkar. He was happy that of all the persons he was the first to know about it.

Savarkar often gave him guidance as to how to read and what to read. Nathuram had now begun to participate in public meetings on political issues.

The Rashtriya Swayamsevak Sangh (R.S.S.) started by its founder, Dr. Hedgewar, with the intention to organise the Hindus, was fast gaining popularity. Nathuram had come to know about this organization.

The attitude of the Muslim community as a whole towards the struggle for attaining independence was clearly seen to be, even at that time, somewhat indifferent and at times even blatantly hostile.

A branch of the R.S.S. was opened at Sangli headed by Shri Kashinathpant Limaye. Nathuram began to take part in the Sangh activities most assiduously. Very soon he came to head its academic department (as '*Bandhik Karyawaha*').

In 1937 the Cooper-Jamnadas Ministry set Veer Savarkar completely free. On his way to Bombay he was felicitated at Kolhapur, Miraj, Sangli, Pune and other places and at each of these places he delivered lectures. Nathuram started going along with Veer Savarkar every where, and then he began to realise how gigantic the task of organising Hindus into a homogeneous whole was, and also how the work of the Sangh (R.S.S.) required to be supplemented by an uprising in the political field. His vision began to widen, and he felt that Sangli was too small place for his activities. He settled in Pune.

The Hindu Mahasabha decided in 1938 to launch an agitation for the removal of injustice done to the Hindus of the Hyderabad State so that they may get their legitimate rights. The name of that agitation was given 'unarmed resistance'.

Nathuram led the first batch of the passive resistance. He and his companions were sentenced to one year's imprisonment, which they underwent in the Hyderabad prison.

Nathuram decided to start a newspaper for the 'Hindu Mahasabha.' It was 'Agrani', some years later was renamed as 'Hindu Rashtra'.

Securities were repeatedly demanded from this newspaper. After the publication of the last issue on the 31st of January 1948, this newspaper went out of publication.

The period of six to seven years prior to 1948 was a very busy period in Nathuram's life. Taken up by the writing of articles for the newspapers, lectures, tours and various odd things he had to do for running the newspaper; taking stock of articles to be written. It should suffice to say for the present that Nathuram had wholly devoted himself to the work of Hindu-sangathan *i.e.* bringing about the solidarity of the Hindus.

Nathuram was peaceful and generous by disposition. On the political platform however he gave full vent to his feelings which at times seemed to reach thc extreme limits of endurance and yet were restrained with effort.

Nathuram could play ably on the harmonium. He played equally well on the flute.

Nathuram was not unfamiliar with the activities started by Gandhiji for mass awakening, nor was he unmindful of their importance. So it would be enlightening to see in what state of mind he took the decision to assassinate Gandhiji.

Those who consider the episode of Gandhiji's assassination as a casual act of a trigger-happy person are ignorant, because they are innocent victims of a propaganda.

Gandhiji by the technic of his Satyagraha conveyed to the common masses the real significance of the words, 'our country bondage', 'Swaraj' etc.

The growing generation at the height of Gandhiji's political career was nourished with the enlivening doses of the songs of independence on their lips.

Armed revolution was never the creed of Gandhiji. But the political Consciousness among the people who were so keen that they freely shouted *'Sardar Bhagat Singh ki jai'* when they were out on mass awakening campaigns.

It is true that many Congress leaders felt that the policy of Gandhiji on the communal problem had fired back and so he should retire from active politics and should not meddle with national decisions.

Severe, of course, were the feelings of the refugees. Independence? Of what worth? Such was the miserable condition they found themselves that the very earth under their feet had literally slipped away without any earthquake having taken place. Waves after waves of blood-drenched refugees returned to India every day.

Every displaced person was himself or herself a grievous wound and actually had a tongue. No newspaper could have succeeded in fanning discontent and indignation and surcharge the whole atmosphere with intense feeling even if it meant to, so poignantly and on such a vast, scale as did every sign and word form the innumerable tongues of the refugees.

Countless people pronounced bitter curses, not only in their private homes, but in public places, that it was because of Gandhiji that they had lost their homes and hearths and so Gandhiji must not live. However the idea of killing Gandhiji was itself far more grievous and repugnant.

It was draining a drought of potent poison. Can you imagine how difficult it was for Nathuram to make up his mind to assassinate Gandhiji as a dire duty and ominous obligation ?

To stand before the world with one's whole past life raised completely to dust and to suffer every sort of indignity, contempt and humiliation from the world over was more appalling and unbearable than self-immolation. So one can very well see that this assassination was not a whimsical act of an inveterate monomaniac shooting at his will.

It is obvious, therefore, that there must be a potent cause or a chain of causes which provoked Nathuram's mind to such an extremity as to deny earthly existence to Gandhiji, and as a consequence thereof to himself.

Nathuram had, at least, the satisfaction that he was not considered to be a maniac, suffering from any morbidity.

Nathuram told an incident:

I had reached the gates of the Birla Bhavan at about ten minutes to five in the evening. The guards at the gates were closely watching the people going in for the prayer-meeting. I was to expect the greatest danger from these guards. So taking utmost precaution to let it appear that I belonged to a group of four or five people going in I managed to enter the Birla Bhavan. Once again I felt that the Police-men moving about had, as it were, focussed their eyes on me, because the prayer-ground was still almost empty. So I hastened as quickly as possible to the spot where people were standing in greater number and stationed myself there.

At about five minutes past five I saw Gandhiji and his entourage leaving the room and approaching the prayer-ground. I went and stood amongst a group of people near the spot where he would ascent the steps to the prayer-ground.

Gandhiji ascended the steps and proceeded five or six steps forward, his hands resting on the shoulders of two girls.

I opened the safety-catch of the pistol inside the pocket itself. I had already observed that in spite of the people round about Gandhiji I could get the scope I wanted.

I needed about three seconds more to go ahead two steps, get in front of Gandhiji, to draw the weapon out of my pocket, and to make obeisance to Gandhiji for whatever useful service he had rendered to the country and the sacrifice he had made in his life-time thereof.

Of the two girls accompanying Gandhiji one was rather too close to him and I feared that she might be hurt in the attempt. So deciding what to do to avoid that eventuality I moved forward and uttering the words 'Namaste' (Bow to you) I bowed to Gandhiji with the hands holding the weapon. Moving one step more ahead I pushed that girl aside.

In the next split second the shots were fired. Weak as he already was, Gandhiji collapsed almost instantly dead on the ground, with the faintest 'Ah'[1] which arose from deep down his lungs.

Gandhiji's indestructible incombustible and under-changeable soul which was also incapable of being dried, was fast leaving the body and vanishing into the elements and I was entering my live Samadhi (living death).

I had a weapon in my hand. I had fired the bullets. Nobody could confidently say that I would not fire some more bullets. If some armed policeman had fired a bullet into me at that moment, it would have been undoubtedly justifiable.

No sooner had the bullets been fired than I raised my hand holding the pistol and shouted 'Police, Police'. Half a minute elapsed, yet no one dared approach nearer. Every moment the strain on my mind was increasing, and I became absolutely restless. I think I was getting excited.

At that time I was not at all conscious whether any body was or was not going to hammer me, nor had I in my mind the slightest thought of warding off the blows if somebody offered to belabour me.

1. The words *'Hey Ram, Hey Ram* and *Hey Ram'* were a fiction of the imagination of the then Government and attributed to him in order to gain the Hindu sentiment.

Today I can interpret my mental condition as existed at that moment. I was prepared to face any consequences of the act of assassinating Gandhiji. Only I did not want to have three charges to be levelled against me by anybody. First, I did not want anyone even to hint that I tried to run away. Half a minute later I again shouted 'Police, Police' I could very well see standing right before me the policemen in uniform, and they dared not step forward to arrest me. Were I to throw away my pistol (to dispel their fear), that act of mine would have been taken to mean that I was preparing a loophole for my defence. Naturally, I did not want such an allegation made against me. And I was at a loss to know how to convince the Police, that I wanted to surrender myself, weapon in hand, to them.

I did not want to hurt any one else even through mistake. That is why I continued to wait for the police to come forward, with my hand holding the pistol raised high up. If I had kept my hand down playing with pistol—though quite inadvertently—there would certainly have been some witnesses to state that I had pointed the pistol at them.'

I started glancing all around and probably met the gaze of Amarnath or that of the so-called soldier. He seemed to be convinced of the sincerity in my eyes and came near to me and held my raised wrist up. He must have felt the total absence of resistance in it. The strain on my mind quickly vanished, and I heaved a sigh of relief. Followed yet another man,, who got hold of my weapon which I let go without any resistance.

And thereafter people drew close to me and encircled me. Some struck me with their hands.

The police were stupid enough to allow the pistol to change hands to satisfy the curious. Some one from the crowd levelled it at me, saying 'With this very pistol I will kill you'. Calmly but loudly enough to make my words audible to him even in that tumultuous noise, I replied, 'With pleasure. Go ahead' But you don't seem to have any knowledge of the way to handle a pistol. Mind, the safety-catch is on. Even if by chance it were to receive the slightest jerk you would likely kill somebody else. Remember, there are some bullets in it.' Then I requested the nearest police officer to take the pistol in his custody, reminding him that the safety-catch was on and there was every likelihood that the man would kill somebody else instead of me. The officer immediately took possession of that pistol, closed the safety-catch and deposited it in his pocket.

Nathuram had already decided at the very outset of the trial not to allow his advocate to cross-examine the witnesses put up to depose in respect of the events of the 30th of January, to the extent, of course, to which they referred to that event.

Many eye-witnesses were examined. Nathuram admired their enthusiasm but pitied their 'honesty'. Everyone wanted the credit of apprehending him. Their deposition was inconsistent and contradictory to one another's.

Nathuram had with him an automatic pistol with seven bullets. He had pulled the trigger only once. Two or three bullets had passed.

Lt. Col. B.L. Taneja, Addl. Civil Surgeon, Irwin Hospital, New Delhi, gave in the course of his evidence the description of the five wounds on Gandhiji's body, and said that in his opinion the death was caused by the bullets from the pistol. He too was not cross-examined. .

This theoretical stand of Nathuram was seen by the East Punjab High Court of the appellants, say their Lordships in their judgment:

> Nathuram V. Godse has not challenged his conviction under Section 302 of the Indian Penal Code for the offence of the murder of Mahatma Gandhi on 30th January, 1948, nor has he appealed from the sentence of death passed on him in respect of that offence. He has confined his appeal and also his arguments at the Bar - he personally argued his appeal, I must say with conspicuous ability evidencing a mastery of facts which would have done credit to any counsel, only to the other charges which have been proved against him.

On an argument relating to the incidence of 20th January, Justice Achhru Ram said:

> We have seen quite enough of Nathuram during the period of more than five-weeks while we were hearing these appeals and particularly during the eight or nine days while he was arguing his own case and we cannot imagine that a man of his calibre could have even entertained the idea (of remaining behind).

The judges had evidently realised that this murder had been an unfortunate outcome of the situation then prevailing in the country. The High Court in the city of Lahore had been turned into a refuge for the Hindus in that city and in that State had been removed perforce and they had to flee for safety to the rest of the Indian territory. If sentencing Nathuram to death was doing justice to the people, then equally so was the just evaluation of his feelings.

Coffee was his favourite drink. He never took tea since his adolescence. While in the condemned cell he once told the Jailor jocularly, 'I don't mind the gallows; but I must have a cup of coffee before the execution.' The manner in which he climbed the execution rope and the words uttered by him have been described earlier. Such was the man called Nathuram V. Godse.

Strange are the ways of life. Nathuram V. Godse's post assassination moves and the stand before the Court being what it was, the Government, for their own political mileage, even bestowed a *Kirti Chakra* upon one Dev Raj Singh for having 'apprehended' Godse. The High Court finding was that Nathuram had made no attempt to run away.

2. **Narayan Dattatraya Apte** *(Accused No. 2)* was born in 1911. He was popularly known as Nana. Nana's four brothers, Balwant, Vishnu, Madhav, and Manohar, were all well occupied in their own separate professions. Manohar had also been abroad for his higher education.

After obtaining his B.Sc., Degree, Nana accepted a teacher's job at Ahmednagar. During his stay at Ahmednagar he was married to Shri Phadtare's daughter.

At Ahmednagar his innate skill and deep interest in teaching attracted pupils to the private tuition classes he conducted. He appeared for his B.T. examination and got his degree.

Endowed with a fair complexion and chiselled features, with a body slightly tender-built, the ever smiling Nana was known in his friends circle to be eminently fitted for a female role.

Faith in and loyalty to Hinduism are seen to be inherent at least in the cultured families of Maharashtra. .So Nana too was nurtured under these traditional domestic influences.

Nana's organizing ability and skill were fast developing, while his contact with Nathuram was maturing through the sessions of the Hindu Mahasabha and gradually both of them came to realise that the other possessed some rare qualities. So towards the early part of 1944 they both planned to start a daily, called 'Agrani'. Nana became the manager of the daily, while Nathuram its editor. This manager-editor relation of these two was to remain steadfast till the end.

The Government of the time used to get exasperated with the Hindu Mahasabha policy of fostering loyalty to Hindutwa amongst the Hindus, because the Congress Ministries followed the policy of appeasement of the Muslims. Security deposits were demanded from 'Agrani' in quick succession.

While Gandhiji was staying at Panchagani, a group of about twenty-five young men led by Nana staged a protest against Gandhiji's policies on 22nd July 1944.

Nana planned and executed another such demonstration before Gandhiji when he was staying in the sweepers' colony in Delhi, with the object of telling him personally not to make any donation to the Muslims at the cost of the Hindus, for such a donation was not going to appease them; not to accept the partition of India; and to learn a lesson from the massacre of the Hindus at Noakhali. Gandhiji's former pledges had all proved futile and the land had been vivisected.

Nana Apte had made a separate Will expressing therein, among other things, the desire to immerse his remains in the Sindhu river, just as Nathuram had done.

On an occasion Nana said to Gopal, 'Look, Gopal, from the point of view of the deceased it is absolutely immaterial how his or her dead body or the ashes are disposed of! But the survivors of the deceased are anxious to honour his or her feelings. We do not have a blind faith in our scriptures. True, we do customarily immerse our mortal remains into the Ganga. But don't we regard all the rivers of India, such equally sacred? Remember, our death is of a political—more particularly of a national character; as such it is but natural that we should cherish feelings of loyalty to our nation. But now that you have posed this question before us, I must answer it satisfactorily. There are two sores which constantly rankle in our hearts.

> This new-born state of Pakistan is a parasite weed that has grown rancorously on the land of the Hindus sucking their vital life-stream,' thundered Nana with passionate indignation. 'No sooner did it receive the nourishment of independence and separate existence, it has started inflicting insults on the rest of India. We have restricted our remark to things that concern us, because that is our limit. May I ask which of all the nations of the world has insulted Gandhiji after his death ?
>
> Which one ?
>
> It's none other than Pakistan! Do you remember the condolence message, sent by Jinnah?'
>
> Yes quite well. A leader of the Hindus has passed away.
>
> Isn't it a great insult to Gandhiji ? How ?
>
> Was it not Jinnah's duty to show gratitude to the man at-least after his death—who for the whole of his life suppressed the aspirations only to foster

by his connivance and concessions the fissiparous and aggressive designs of the Muslims in India in the vain hope of bringing about the Hindu Muslim unity ? Had he called - and he did call - Gandhiji to be such a leader before the birth of Pakistan, it wouldn't have amounted to an insult to him. For that would have been looked upon as Jinnah's political ruse to achieve his end. That is why we earnestly desire that only after the state where Gandhiji was insulted as a 'Hindu' is brought under our control with the whole of the river Indus, the Sindhu, watering the territories under the sway of India, should our remains be immersed in it—the sacred river of ours—ours from the very hoary past.

Shri Shreeprakash was the then Indian High Commissioner in Pakistan, who complained with tears in his voice that the Government of Pakistan didn't allow the immersion of Gandhiji's ashes into the river Indus. The immersion of Gandhiji's ashes into the river Indus was purely a matter of sentiment—and more particularly a matter of Hindu sentiment. How could they then tolerate the holy water of a holy river in their holy land to be polluted by the ashes of a Hindu?

'We fondly hoped,' continued Nana, 'that our Government would preserve one urn containing Gandhiji's ashes to be immersed into the river Indus when it was possible for it to do so. But we swallowed that insulting refusal of Pakistan quite sheepishly.'

Nana had told his wife, Soubhagyavati Champutai, 'If you believe in the immortality of the soul, then you are and will remain

Soubhagyavati even after my death! Move about in the society wearing your external symbols of your Soubhagya.[2] Soubhagyavati Champutai works as a teacher in the Kindergarten School conducted by the Rani Lakshmibai Smarak Mandal.

3. **Vishnu Ramkrishna Karkare** *(Accused No. 3)* had a lodging and boarding house at Ahmednagar. He was an active worker. When Noakhali in Bengal (now in Bangala Desh) had become the slaughter house of the Hindus, Karkare, with a batch of ten there to mobilise the Hindus and adopt a militant posture in their defence. He had raised a number of shelter camps under the Hindu Mahasabha banner. This was in 1946-47. Vishnu Karkare continued his business at Ahmednagar till he expired of heart attack on April 6, 1974. His wife looks after the business.

4. **Madan Lal Pahwa** (*Accused No. 4*), who had exploded the gun-cotton slab, was a refugee. He was a witness to the awful events of massacre, loot and arson. Carvans, miles together in length and comprising lakhs of humans, driven out of the hearths and homes, were on their way to truncated India. Madan Lal has narrated his poignant sufferings in his statement before the Court.

2. 'Soubhagyavati' precedes the name of a married Hindu woman whose husband is alive. *Mangala Sootra,* a kind of necklace of a particular design, around the neck and a *Kumkum* Tilak i.e. a red mark on the forehead are worn by such a woman, customarily in Maharashtra and in the South.

Madan Lal who married after his release manages purchase and sale for some paper mills in Bombay.

5. **Shankar Kistaiya** *(Accused No. 5)* served Digambar Badge, the approver (as a personal/domestic servant). He expired a few years after his acquittal.

6. **Gopal Godse** *(Accused No. 6.)* The younger brother of Nathuram Godse. He had been charged with conspiracy on the allegation that he was present at the Birla House on January 20. So was convicted for abetment and sentenced to transportation for life. He was born on 12th June 1920.

7. **Digambar Badge** *(Accused No. 7)*, Digambar Badge was originall Accused No. 7, but he formally turned approver. No. 7 was allotted to Savarkar. Digambar Badge was a Hindu Sanghatanist and a dealer in arms. He had a conviction that Hindus should be armed in the pockets in which they were in minority and should be able to retailiate in case of attack from the Muslims. The prosecution claimed that it was Badge who had supplied the gun-cotton slab ignited by Madan Lal. A hand grenade too was recovered from Madan Lal. Some more ammunition was recovered from Badge.

After his discharge from the custody Digambar Badge was given service in the Police Department. He has since retired.

8. **Vinayak Damodar Savarkar** *(Accused No. 8).* Out of the nine accused produced before the Special Court, Red Fort, Delhi, in the Gandhi Murder Case, Swatantryaveer Vinayak Damodar Savarkar was originally Accused No. 8. As mentioned before, on the 27th May 1948 all the accused were brought before the Special Court for the first time. Digambar Ramchandra Badge, accused No. 7, had turned an Approver. So he was formally removed from the docks and consequently the numbers of the other accused moved up. Savarkar therefore became accused No. 7.

Vinayak Damodar Savarkar was born on 28.5.1883 at Bhagoor, a village near Nasik, a district town in Maharashtra. Nasik is famous for its religious importance. As Savarkar birth place, Bhagoor too became a shrine for the devotees of Swaraj. Vinayak's father Damodar was a landlord in its humble meaning. Vinayak had an elder brother by the name Ganesh and a younger one called Narayan. Vinayak's mother Radha was a household lady.

Vinayak had a sharp memory. He could recite verses with little effort. This formed the basis for him to compose poetry in subsequent years. From the childhood itself, Vinayak showed a tendency of organising boys of his age and engaging them in the programmes for liberation of the country from the British yoke. He had named the groups as *'Mitra Mela'* (gathering of friends).

At Bhagoor was a Deity; Goddess Bhagwati having eight arms. Vinayak, who was hardly fifteen years of age, vowed before the Goddess that he would take a fight against the Britishers to overthrow them and in that course he would fight to the last drop of his blood.

Vinayak had his primary education at Bhagoor and then at Nasik. After matriculation he went to Pune and joined Ferguson College. He continued his organisational work at Pune too, among the college students. On occasions he consulted the then leaders like Lokmanya Tilak and Shivram Mahadev Paranjpe.

In 1906, Vinayak organised a bonfire of foreign clothes in Pune. It was the first act of open revolt against the purchase of the British goods.

Vinayak graduated himself from the Ferguson College. He desired to go to England for the study of Law and become a barrister. A scholarship was sponsored by Pandit Shaymjee Krishna Varma. Lokmanya Tilak recommended Vinayak for the scholarship.

Vinayak reached England and here he had a broader field now to plant patriotism in the youths from different provinces. Besides he wrote for 'Kal' a periodical of S.M. Paranjpe. The language of his news letters was fiery, and yet written skillfully.

Madan Lal Dhingra, the youth who shot dead Corzen Waily on 22nd June 1909, was sentenced to death. The statement found in Madan Lal Dhingra's pocket was suppressed by the police. Savarkar arranged its publication in a daily a day before Madan Lal Dhingra's execution, i.e. on 16th August 1909. The title was 'Challenge' meaning that the Police should say as to whether or not this was the statement they had seized from Madan Lal Dhingra upon his arrest. Madan Lal Dhingra was executed at Bristol prison on 17th August 1909.

In India, Anant Kanhere, a 17 years old boy, assassinated the Collector of Nasik, Mr. Jackson, on 22nd December, 1909. Savarkar was arrested in London on 13.3.1910 and brought to India to face trial for this case.

On the way, at Marseilles in France, Savarkar jumped from the ship and went to the shore, but he was apprehended and taken back to the ship.

Savarkar, along with thirtyfour others, was charged with sedition. On 24.12.1910 he was sentenced to transportation for life. He was also charged with participation in Jackson assassination case. On 30.1.1911 he was again sentenced to transportation for life. The sentences were ordered to run consecutively.

Savarkar was transported to Andamans—(Kala Pani) on 1.7.1911 where he remained for ten years. In May 1921 Vinayak was brought back and lodged in Yeravada (Pune) Jail for about three years. On 6.1.1924 Vinayak was shifted to Ratnagiri and lodged there with some restrictions until 1937 when he was finally released.

Since the day Savarkar was released from the detention at Ratnagiri, Savarkarism and Gandhism came to grips openly. In addition to his life-mission of attaining national independence, now Savarkar had to undertake another programme of refuting this lopsided principle of non-violence; which was dinned into the people's ears day in and day out. The constructive aspect of Savarkar's programme was organizing the Hindus—'Hindu-Sanghatan'.

The Hindu Mahasabha was a new entrant in the field of Indian politics. Savarkar was elected as the President of the Hindu Mahasabha to preside over the session at Karnavati i.e. Ahmedabad, held in December 1937.

Savarkar had a strong foresight. His call to the young Indians to join the British army with a view to learn the techniques of the modern warfare and the modern weapons and not to lose the God sent opportunity of being war—worthy and equipped them with arms; leaving to the opportune time to teach them against whom these arms were to be used. It was deliberately and mischievously distorted and ridiculed by the Congress with its well set up propaganda machinery, which could very easily publish in a perverse manner that the Hindu Mahasabha was anti-independence, that it was revisionist and retrograde.

As early as 1942, in his Kanpur address, Savarkar had predicted that the Congress was going to vivisect the country and warned the nation against it. And, five years later, it came true.

On 15th August 1947 independence was achieved. To acknowledge this victory Veer Savarkar hoisted the pan-Hindu Flag of the Hindu Maha Sabha at the top of his house and also the accepted National Flag with three colours and the Ashok Chakra at its centre.

Veer Savarkar had desired that since the Hindus were being thrown out of the territory now known as Pakistan, the Muslims from the rest of India should not be prevented from going to Pakistan which was their own creation. He was watchful of the events and prophetic in his utterances. Vinayak Damodar Savarkar came to be known as Swatantrya Veer because of his ceaseless efforts and sufferings, boldness and courage, guidance and advice for achieving Swaraj.

Gandhiji was assassinated on 30.1.1948. On the next day, large scale arrests of Hindu leaders and others commenced. In the ensuing few weeks as many as 10,000 persons were arrested under the Preventive Detention Act. All of them, were only Hindus. Savarkar's house was searched. Files and papers were seized for scrutiny. While Savarkar remained in preventive detention, his family friends and associates were kept under surveillance.

One can safely infer that prior to the independence, the Congress Government under Pandit Nehru's leadership was examining how to ensure their survival in power after independence. After the assassination, which was little over five months after independence, they were quick to gauge the general Hindu sentiment. They had to proceed about their task to ensure their survival with a little more care. For that two things were considered by them as necessary:

(i) divide the Hindus on caste lines.

(ii) appease the Muslims.

Savarkar had always a firm preachment that there could be no distinguishing between one Hindu and another on caste lines and there should be no appeasement of any section or community for political gains. Therefore, they decided that instead of giving an 'Award' to Veer Savarkar, for his contribution towards India's independence, they should implicate him in the Gandhi murder case so that his arrest, pending trial coupled with diversion of energies towards defence of the case, could give them a much needed breather to carry out their aforesaid object of dividing the Hindus on caste lines, appeasing the Muslims and also try and put forward their own confidants (sycophants) as ostensible Hindu leaders. The object being to somehow shift the Hindu focus from one man to several persons of their own installation.

Since a thorough search of the papers seized from Veer Savarkar's house, (documents and correspondence dating from 1938 and running into 143 files with 10,000 papers), and other investigations did not reveal anything incriminating, they used third degree method against Badge, promised him pardon and the result was that police had a statement from Badge implicating Savarkar. Later on, therefore, the arrest of Savarkar was converted from one under Preventive Detention Act to an accused in the

Gandhi Murder case. The trial took its time and effort and all this while Savarkar remained in prison. A year later, the day of the judgment dawned. Savarkar was acquitted.

A huge crowd of people had assembled to greet Savarkar outside Red Fort. The exonerated Savarkar was stepping out of the historic Red Fort. The oceanlike crowd was visibly moved and it embraced Savarkar with the sky-rending shouts of:

Swatantrya Lakshmi Ki Jai!

(Victory of the Goddess of Freedom)

Akhand Bharat Amar Rahe!

(Long live Undivided India)

Swatantryaveer Savarkar Ki Jai!

(Victory to Swa. Savarkar)

Veer Savarkar had inaugurated the Calcutta Session of the Hindu Maha Sabha after his release in the year 1949, at which Shri N.B. Khare was elected President. After 1950, his ailing health prevented him from taking part in public functions. It was only on rare occasions, that he addressed public meetings.

In 1957, he addressed the gathering in Delhi to commemorate the centenary of the first War of Independence fought in 1857. His speech was touching. He said:

> *you have followed me so far in spite of the fact that in return you did not get any honour or wealth. What you got in return was imprisonment, gallows, hatred from the people and curses from the secularists. And yet you did not forsake this path and followed it to the end with all your might. This spirit of yours will certainly lead the Hindus to achieve their cultural independence.*

In subsequent years he delivered lectures on Hindu History. They have been compiled as 'Six Glorious Epoches.'

The people felicitated Veer Savarkar in the year 1960, and named the occasion as *'Mrityunjaya Din.'* If two consecutive punishments of transportation for life were to be executed in his case he was to see the free world in that year. As Savarkar outlived the scheduled release year, the occasion was named as 'Mrityunjaya' (one who over-powered the deity of Death).

In the beginning of February 1966 while running his 83rd year, Savarkar decided that soul ought to be freed from the human body. He gave up food and confined himself to meditation. Before that, he had written:

> *I have done everything possible with my humble strength for the sake of my people, nation. However life has its own limitation. When the limbs could no more be burdened with any task, surrender to Nature is the only honourable way. Let me be free now from the wrapper of the body I possess.*

Veer Savarkar breathed his last on Feb. 26, 1966, at Bombay, ironically, after suffering the rigours of sentences and detention both during the British Rule and also when India was free. His fault:

> *He fought for independence of India, opposed the vivisection and the vivisectionists, urged for just rights for the Hindus, and countered the division of Hindus on caste lines.*

Many of his statements have been compiled in a book by Shri G.M. Joshi and Balarao Savarkar. The book is called 'Historic Statements by V.D. Savarkar'.

A word more about him. The freedom struggle was no single man's effort. It was a collective effort of thousands, and of the millions who were behind those thousands. Savarkar was one of them. He is, however, in one sense more fortunate, for Savarkar's soul has been spared the indignation of false claims to credit by the politicians of today, for what were his sacrifices. It is sad to see that credit for the sacrifice made by many a genuine national patriotic figure, be it Bhagat Singh, Uttam Chand, Madan Lal Dhingra, Khudi Ram, Rash Behari or even Subhash Chandra Bose, who were not only patriots in the true sense, but men of values and principles, is claimed and used by the today's politicians to project themselves as heirs to their nobel legacy. Twisted propaganda and sham functions are all orchestrated towards basking in their reflected glory and seeking to present themselves as a chip of the same block, before a nation which has been a calculated victim of little education and social divisions.

It is because Savarkar was too well known and his writings too profuse, that his contributions have been spared such misuse. The day when he was jailed and the day when he was released, or even his birth or death anniversary, all go without politically sponsored public meetings addressed by politicians wearing Gandhi caps, and followed by a long coverage on the Television/ Doordarshan and the Radio. At least this ensures that his soul rests in peace.

9. Dr. Dattatraya Sadashiv Parchure (Accused No. 9) was a qualified doctor. He practised at Gwalior. He was an able organiser. He met attacks by the Muslims by counter attacks. He was involved on the charge that Nathuram obtained the pistol from him. A confession was extracted from him under pressure. The High Court acquitted him. He was married and stayed in his own house with his family. He expired in the year 1986.

There were three more accused cited by the prosecution. They were **Gangadhar Dandavate, Gangadhar Jadhao and Surya Dev Sharma,** all from Gwalior. They were declared absconders. Their prosecution depended on Dr. Parchure's conviction. Dr. Parchure was acquitted by the High Court on 22nd June 1949. The three thereafter surrendered themselves to the police, the police produced them before the local Magistrate, who discharged them of any prosecution.

❑

The Will

The Will of Nathuram is in the form of a letter in Hindi, addressed to Shri Dattatraya Vinayak Godse, his younger brother. The Magistrate put a seal over it on November 15, 1949. The Jail authorities passed on the letter to Shri Dattatraya.

Nathuram left behind only valuable property-his ashes and instructed how to dispose them of. The will was in Hindi and an English translation there of appears on the next page.

My dear Dattatraya,

If you are allowed to perform last rites of my body you may perform them in any manner. But I am to express herewith a specific wish.

The river Indus (Sindhu), on the banks of which our pre-historic Rishis composed the Vedas is the boundary of our Bharatvansha i.e. Hindusthan.

My ashes may be sunk in the Holy Sindhu river when she will again flow freely under the aegis of the flag of Hindusthan. That will be the sacred day for us.

It hardly matters even if it took a couple of generations for realising my wish. Preserve the ashes till then, and if that day would not dawn in your life time, pass on the remains to posterity for translating my desire into reality.

If and when the Government lifts ban on my statement made in the Court, I authorise you to publish it.

14.11.1949 Nathuram Vinayak Godse

I have donated Rs. 101/- on this day for its utilisation for the dome (Kalasha) of the sacred Somnath temple which is under construction.

15.11.1949 NathuramVinayak Godse
7.15 a.m Seal of The Magistrate
signature and date
15-11-1949

From Justice G.D. Khosla's Memoirs*

Nathuram Godse shot at Mahatma Gandhi, while he was going to his prayer meeting in Birla House at 5:00 P.M. on 30 January, 1948. Gandhiji fell down on the spot and succumbed to his injuries within a few minutes. Godse voluntarily surrendered to the police and was taken in to custody. He was kept at Tughlaq Road police station for a few days.

During investigation it was observed that Godse was not the only person concerned, in this murder. There was a deep conspiracy behind the murder. After five months the Police declared the case ripe for trial.

The trial began on 22 June, 1948 inside the Historic Red Fort of Delhi, before Mr. Justice Atma Charan, a senior member of the judicial branch of the Indian Civil Service. The court was open to the pubic.

The eight persons charged with murder, conspiracy to commit murder and offences punishable under the Arms and Explosive Substances Act were:

1. Nathuram Godse, *37, Editor, 'Hindu Rashtra', Poona.*
2. Gopal Godse, *27, Storekeeper, Army Depot, Poona.*
3. Narayan Apte,*34,Managing Director, Hindu Rashtra Prakashan Ltd*
4. Vishnu Karkare, *37, Restaurant Proprietor, Ahmad Nagar.*
5. Madanlal Pahwa,*20, Refugee Camp, Ahmad Nagar.*
6. Shankar Kistayya, *27, Domestic Servant, Poona.*

---

* Source: 'G.D.KHOSLA- THE MURDER OF THE MAHATMA And Other Cases From a Judge's Notebook'- 1977, JAICO PRESS PVT LTD. BOMBAY

Justice G. D. Khosla

The Chief Justice of India decided to constitute a bench of three judges to hear the appeal by Godse and his accomplices. The judges were Justice Bhandar, Justice Achhruram and Justice G. D. Khosla.

7. Dattataraya Parchure, *49, Medical Practitioner, Gwalior.*
8. Vinayak Savarkar, *65, Barrister-at-Law, Landlord and Property Owner, Bombay.*

The advocate General Mr. C.K. Daphtary opened the prosecution case on 24 June, 1948 and the examination of the witnesses began.

Digambar Badge (pronounced Bahdgay), became the approver in this case. He was alleged to be co conspirator in the murder plan of Mahatma Gandhi. He was tendered conditional pardon.

The examination of the witnesses concluded on 6 November 1948. On 10 February, 1949, the trial court pronounced its judgment. Savarkar was acquitted. Nathuram Godse and Narayan Apte were sentenced to death and the remaining five accused were awarded sentences of imprisonment for life.

Four days after the judgment was passed, Godse appealed in the High Court claiming that there was no conspiracy and he was the only one responsible for the murder. The appeals for other accused persons were also filed in the High Court.

Considering the importance of the case the Chief Justice appointed three judges instead of two for the appeal to be heard by the divisional bench. The judges were Mr. Justice Bhandari, Mr. Justice Achhruram and Mr. Justice G.D. Khosla..

Punjab High Court at Simla was hurriedly set up during the autumn of 1948 in a large memorial building called 'Peterhoff' which was the summer residence of the Viceroy. Admission to the court was regulated by the passes issued by the Registrar for security reason and limit the number of persons. All the advocates who were not engaged in arguing their cases before other judges had occupied the seats in the front row. Behind them the gentry of Simla occupied the chairs. There were separate seats for pressmen. On the right of the dais some seats were reserved for V.I.P's who were the wives of Hon'ble Judges and high Government officials. In front of the dais, advocates representing the appellants were sitting. On the right hand end of the front row sat four lawyers for the prosecution.

Nathuram Godse had declined to be represented by a lawyer and wished to argue his case himself as he could not afford the fee of an advocate. Though his request to argue on the basis of poverty appeared to be an excuse. His prayer was granted. He was standing in a specially constructed dock. The real reason was to show himself as a fearless patriot and a passionate protagonist of Hindu ideology.

Brief introduction of the accused persons

Nathuram was the son of a village postmaster. He had three brothers and two sisters and was the second child. At 22, he joined Rashtriya Swayam Sewak Sangh and Hindu Mahasabha. The aim of these organizations was to protect Hindu culture and solidarity. Later on, he started a newspaper 'AGRANI' and subsequently changed its name to 'HINDU RASHTRA'. Godse had made a deep study of 'Bhagavad-Gita' and knew most of its verses by heart. He used to quote these verses to justify acts of violence to achieve a righteous aim. He had not married.

Gopal Godse was the younger brother of Nathuram Godse. He was not as passionate about the Hindu cause as his brother. He had two daughters. He like Nathuram was also a member of Hindu Mahasabha. He joined the army and was appointed a store keeper at Kirkee near Poona. During the war he went to Iraq and Iran. He was influenced by Savarkar's views, which were against any proposal to divide India. Nathuram Godse dissuaded him to join him, as he was a married man with responsibilities. Gopal Godse thought over the matter and in the end joined his brother.

Narayan Dattatraya Apte, a Brahmin, was B.Sc. and was a teacher at Ahmednagar School. He started a rifle club and joined Hindu Rashtra Dal. During this period he met Godse and became his friend. In 1943 he joined Indian Air Force and was awarded a king's Commission. Four months later, he resigned from his job as his younger brother had died and he had to look after the family now. Though he did not possess Godse's religious fervor, yet he got convinced that nothing could be achieved in politics through peaceful means.

Vishnu Ramakrishnan Karkare's parents were very poor and were unable to support him. They left him at an orphanage and abandoned him. He ran away and supported himself by working in Hotels and restaurants and finally started his own restaurant in Ahmednagar. He became an active member of Hindu Mahasabha and was elected secretary of the district branch. There, he met Apte and the two became friends. He contested Ahmednagar Municipal Committee election and got elected. In 1946, he went to Noakhali with a relief party to assist the victims of Muslim population. He stayed there for about three months. There he witnessed kidnappings and raping of Hindu women. He was quite upset when Mahatma Gandhi said that he had not seen even a single kidnapping or raping of Hindu women and awarded Rs. 10000/- to a vicious criminal Ghulam Sarwar an M.L.A., who was responsible for these crimes.

Madanlal Pahwa, a refugee from Pakpattan (now in Pakistan) ran away from school. He went to Poona and joined the Army. During training he asked for and was given release orders. Large scale rioting had started, when he reached home. His father and aunt were murdered. He was evacuated to Ferozepur. He came to Poona and came across Apte and Godse. He realized that the Government had no sympathy for Hindus who were victims of the partition and started organizing demonstrations by the group of refugees.

Shanker Kistayya, an illiterate was the son of a village carpenter. He came to Poona in search of a job, where he met Badge, who dealt in daggers, knives and firearms and ammunition. Kistayya started working with him as a domestic servant at a salary of Rs.30/- per month. Kistayya apart from doing Badge's housework used to wash his clothes, looked after his shop and drove his rickshaw. He was Badge's trusted agent for carrying his contraband arms and weapons to his customers. Because of communal trouble in Hyderabad and other parts of the country, there was a great demand of such arms.

Dr. Dattatraya Parchure, a Brahmin from Gwalior was a medical doctor and surgeon. He joined Medical Service but was dismissed in 1934. He began private practice and joined Hindu Mahasabha. He was elected Dictator of the local Hindu Rashtriya Sena. Because of his links with these organizations, he happened to meet Godse and Apte.

Vinayak Savarkar or **Veer Savarkar** was a barrister, poet, play write and historian. He was linked to revolutionaries and was sentenced to imprisonment for fourteen years at cellular Jail in Andaman and Nicobar islands. After his release in 1937, he joined Hindu Mahasabha and devoted himself in its objective for United India. For many years he remained its President.

Digambar Ramchandra Badge, the approver from Challisgaon in East Khandesh was a school dropout came to Poona to earn his livelihood. There he started buying knives, daggers and knuckle dusters from a shop and hawked them. After coming in contact with some Hindu Mahasabha activists, he started selling books, knives, daggers and knuckle dusters at the stall taken in the Hindu Mahasabha's annual sessions, wherever these were held. He met Godse and Apte at Veer Savarkar's house, who was the President of Hindu Mahasabha.

This group of people became united by a common cause which was hatred for Mahatma Gandhi. They learnt that Mahatma Gandhi had started his fast to compel the Government to pay Rupees fifty five crore to Pakistan. After three days the Government surrendered to Mahatma Gandhi's demand. It was too much for them to bear this blackmail of Mahatma Gandhi. They felt till Mahatma Gandhi was alive he would not let the government take any decision independently. On 13 January Godse and Apte hatched a plan to get rid of Gandhiji. The execution of this plan needed forethought team work. The first thing Godse did was to make an assignment of his assets. There were two persons who were closer to him; one was Apte, his friend and business associate and the other one was his younger brother Gopal. They had risked their lives on his bidding. He considered doing whatever was possible for him to do for their families. He was holding two insurance policies of Rs. 2000/- and Rs.3000/-each. He nominated their wives as the beneficiaries.

To execute the plan, Godse and Apte came to Delhi by plane on 17 January and stayed at Marina Hotel till 20 January. Badge and Shankar came to Delhi on 19 January and stayed at Hindu Mahasabha Bhawan. Pahwa and

Karkare had already come on 17 January and were staying at a hotel in Chandni Chowk. On the 20th Morning, Apte, Karkare, Badge and Shankar visited Birla House at Albuquerque Road, now known as Tees January Marg, where prayers meetings of Mahatma Gandhi were held. It was decided that next day Pahwa would explode the gun cotton slab near the back door and they expected a stampede to follow after the explosion. In the ensuing confusion Badge and his servant Shankar would fire at Gandhiji from front and back and each would throw a hand grenade. Gopal Godse, Pahwa and Karkare would also throw hand grenades. Thereafter everyone would escape.

Next day during the prayer speech, Pahwa exploded the guncotton slab near the back door. No stampede occurred, as Gandhiji thought that it was a military practice and asked the audience to calm down and be seated. Pahwa was apprehended and their whole plan got foiled.

All of them went back and met at Thane, a suburb of Bombay. Nathuram mentioned several instances from history and emphasized that a single person's act had better chance to succeed. He took the responsibility to assassinate Gandhiji single handedly.

On 29 January Godse, Apte and Karkare came to Delhi. On 30 January at 4:30 P.M. Godse hired a tonga for Birla House. The other two also followed him. At Birla House about 200 persons had gathered to listen to Gandhiji. Gandhiji as usual was coming up slowly with his hands resting on the shoulders of two girls. As he raised his hands to join them in the customary greeting, Godse took a quick step forward, pushed aside the girl and fired three shots in quick succession. Mahatma Gandhi collapsed and fell down saying 'ah' and died within twenty minutes.

Godse made no attempt to escape and was caught immediately by a police officer. Apte and Karkare came out and returned to Bombay.

The whole country was investigated and the arrests followed very quickly. Badge was arrested on 31 January, Gopal Godse on 5 February and Dr. Parchure from Gwalior on the same day as Gopal Godse. Shankar was arrested on 6 February, Apte and Karkare on 14 February,1948.

At the trial, Godse admitted his crime, but maintained that it was only he who was responsible for Gandhiji's murder and no one else was involved in any conspiracy. He admitted that he and Apte had travelled to Delhi by air on 17 January and stayed at Hotel Marina and he again came on 27 January. He also admitted having visited Dr. Parchure at Gwalior. Apte too admitted that he had travelled with Nathuram Godse to Delhi at both the occasions as well as to Gwalior. Karkare too admitted coming to Delhi on 17 January and staying at Hotel Sharif. He denied his role in the conspiracy. Shankar pleaded to the trial court that he had carried out his master's orders and was ignorant of any conspiracy. Gopal Godse totally denied the charges that he had gone to Delhi on 18 January and was present there up to 20 January. Madanlal Pahwa admitted to his crime but asserted that the act of exploding the gun –cotton slab was to show his resentment of the refugees like himself. He had exploded it at a safe distance from everyone so that no harm is caused by the explosion to anyone.

Judges gave Dr. Parchure and Shankar the benefit of doubt accepting their appeal for acquittal. The conviction and sentence of the remaining appellants were confirmed.

Justice G.D. Khosla one of the Judges on the bench of Punjab High Court in his book 'Murder Of The Mahatma' says : 'The highlight of the appeal before us, was the discourse delivered by Nathuram Godse in his defence. He spoke for several hours, discussing in the first instance, the facts of the case and then the motives which prompted him to take Mahatma Gandhi's life. Following passages taken from this statement will give some indication of his opinion and attitudes.'

"Born in a devotional Brahmin family, I instinctively came to revere Hindu Religion, its History and Hindu culture. I had been intensely proud of Hindudom as a whole. Nevertheless, as I grew up, I developed a tendency to free thinking unfettered by any superstitious allegiance to any 'ism', political or religious. That is why I worked actively for the eradication of untouchability and caste system based on birth alone. I publically joined anti-caste movements and maintained that all Hindus should be treated with equal status as to rights, social and religious, and should be high or low on their merit alone. I used to take part in organized anti-caste dinners in which thousands of Hindus-Brahmins, Kshatriyas, Vaishyas, Chamars and Bhangis broke the caste rules and dined in the company of each other.' Thereafter he explained how Muslim atrocities perpetrated on the Hindus under the patronage of Suhrawardy in Noakhali. .... 'Gandhiji started calling him Shahid Saheb- a martyr soul even in his prayer meetings. ..... Not only that, Mahatma Gandhi in his prayer meetings in temple in Bhangi colony started reading Quran in spite of protests by the Hindu worshippers there. Of course he dared not read Geeta in a Mosque. On 15 August Punjab was set in flames by the Muslims, The Hindu Mahasabha on my insistence decided to boycott the festivities and the Congress Government and to launch a fighting programme to check the Muslim onslaught. Gandhiji in fact succeeded in doing what the

British had always wanted to do in pursuance of their policy of 'Divide and Rule'. He helped them in dividing India and it is not yet certain whether their rule has ceased.

The accumulating provocation of 32 years, culminating in his last pro- Muslim fast, at last, goaded me to the conclusion that the existence of Gandhiji should be brought to an end immediately.

On coming back to India he developed a subjective mentality under which he alone was to be the final judge of what was right or wrong....either the Congress had to surrender its will to his, and had to be content with playing the second fiddle to all his eccentricity, whimsically, metaphysics and primitive vision. Many people thought his politics were irrational, but they had either to withdraw from the Congress or to place their intelligence at his feet to do what he liked with it. In such irresponsibility Gandhiji was guilty of blunder after blunder, failure after failure and disaster after disaster. No one single political victory can be claimed to his credit during 33 years of his political predominance.

So long as Gandhian method was in the ascendance, frustration was the only inevitable result.....As regards non violence, it was absurd to expect 40 crores of people to regulate their lives on such lofty plane and it broke down most conspicuously in 1942. As regards truth, the least I can say is that the truthfulness of the average congressman is by no means of a higher order than that of a man in the street, and that very often it is untruth, masked by a thin veneer of pretended truthfulness.

Gandhiji's inner voice, his spiritual power and his doctrine of non violence, of which so much is made of, all crumbled before Mr. Jinnah's iron will and proved to be powerless. Having known that with his spiritual powers he could not influence Mr. Jinnah, Gandhiji should have either changed his policy or could have admitted his defeat and given way to others of different views to deal with Mr. Jinnah and his Muslim League. But Gandhiji was not honest enough to do that. He could not forget his egoism or self even for the practical policies; while the great blunders-blunders as big as Himalayas were being committed.

Briefly speaking, I thought to myself and foresaw that I shall be totally ruined and the only thing that I could expect from the people would be nothing but hatred and that I shall have lost my honour, even more valuable than my life, if I were to kill"

Nathu Ram Godse requested the Honourable Court not to show any mercy to him or any one on his behalf should beg for mercy towards him and may pass orders of sentence as may be proper. He professed that honest writers of history would weigh his act and find the true value thereof on some day in future.

He ended his narration on a high note of emotional reciting verses from Bhagwadgita and the slogan – *AKHAND BHARAT AMAR RAHE-VANDE MATARAM.*

Mr. Justice Khosla writes in his memoirs— "The audience was visibly and audibly moved. There was a deep silence when he ceased speaking. Many women were in tears and men were coughing and searching for their handkerchiefs. The silence was accentuated and made deeper by the sound of occasional subdued sniff or a muffed cough. It seemed to me that I was taking part in some kind of melodrama or in a scene out of a Hollywood feature film.

I have however no doubt that had the audience of that day been constituted into a jury and entrusted with the task of deciding Godse's appeal, they would have brought in a verdict of 'not guilty,' by an over whelming majority"

The final chapter of this sad story takes us to the Central Gaol, Ambala where Nathuram Godse and Apte were executed on the morning of November 15 , 1949.The two condemned prisoners were led out of their cells with their hands pinioned behind them. Godse walked in front. His step occasionally faltered. His demeanour and general appearance evidenced a state of nervousness and fear. He tried to fight against it and keep up a bold exterior by shouting every few seconds the slogan **'Akhand Bharat'** (undivided India)....... The desperate cry was taken up by Apte, who shouted **'Amar Rahe'** (may stay for ever). His loud and firm tone made an uncanny contrast to Godse's at times almost feeble utterance... A single gallows had been prepared for the execution of both. Two ropes, each with a noose, hung from the high crossbar in parallel lines. Godse and Apte were made to stand side by side, the black cloth bags were drawn over their heads and tied at the necks. After adjusting the nooses, the executioner stepped off the platform and pulled the lever.

... The dead bodies were cremated inside the gaol, the ground where the pyres had been erected was ploughed up and the earth and ashes taken to the Ghaggar river and secretly submerged at a secluded spot."

Justice G.D. Khosla was one of the three judges on the bench of Punjab High Court passing judgment on the persons involved in the case. Some of his narrative thought is a repeat what Godse has already described. Yet for the sake of continuity it could not be avoided.(Editor)

Nathuram Godse

Narayan Apte

Veer Savarkar

Gopal Godse

Vishnu Karkare

Snankar Kistaya

Digambar Badge

Madanlal Pahwa

EPILOGUE

"May It please your honour"

Nathuram Godse - His Last Speech in the Court

[On 8 November 1948, Nathuram Godse rose to make his statement in court. Reading quietly from a typed manuscript, he sought to explain why he had killed Gandhi. His thesis covered ninety-pages, and he was on his feet for five hours. Godse's statement, excerpted below, should be read by citizens and scholars in its entirely, for it provides an insight into his personality and his understanding of the concept of Indian nationhood.]

"Born in a devotional Brahmin family, I instinctively came to revere Hindu religion, Hindu history and Hindu culture. I had, therefore, been intensely proud of Hinduism as a whole. As I grew up I developed a tendency to free thinking unfettered by any superstitious allegiance to any isms, political or religious. That is why I worked actively for the eradication of untouchability and the caste system based on birth alone. I openly joined anti-caste movements and maintained that all Hindus are of equal status as to rights, social and religious, and should be considered high or low on merit alone and not through the accident of birth in a particular caste or profession.

I used publicly to take part in organized anti-caste dinners which thousands of Hindus, Brahmins, Vaishyas, Kshatriyas, Chamars and B-----s participated. We broke the caste rules and dined in the company of each other. I have read the speeches and writings of Dadabhai Naoroji, Vivekanand, Gokhale, Tilak, along with the books of ancient and modern history of India and some prominent countries like England, France, America and Russia. Moreover I studied the tenets of socialism and Marxism. But above all I studied very closely what Veer (brave) Savarkar and Gandhiji had written and spoken, as to my mind these two ideologies have contributed more to the moulding of the thought and action of the Indian people during the last thirty years or so, than any other factor has done.

All this thinking and reading led me to believe that it was my first duty to serve Hindudom and Hindus both as a patriot and as a world citizen. To secure the freedom and to safeguard the just interests of some thirty crores (three hundred million) of Hindus would automatically constitute the freedom and well-being of all India, one fifth of the human race. This conviction led me naturally to devote myself to the Hindu Sanatanist ideology and programme, which alone, I came to believe, could win and preserve the National Independence of Hindustan, my Motherland, and enable her to render true service to humanity as well. Since the year 1920, that is, after the demise of Lokmanya Tilak, Gandhi's influence in the Congress first increased and then became supreme.

His activities for public awakening were phenomenal in their intensity and were reinforced by the slogan of truth and non-violence, which he paraded ostentatiously before the country. No sensible or enlightened person could object to these slogans. In fact there is nothing new or original in them. They are implicit in every constitutional public movement. But it is nothing but a dream if you imagine the bulk of mankind is, or can ever become, capable of scrupulous adherence to these lofty principles in its normal life from day to day. In fact, honour, duty and love of one's own kith and kin and country might often compel us to disregard non-violence and to use force. I could never conceive that an armed resistance to an aggression is unjust.

I would consider it a religious and moral duty to resist and if possible, to overpower such an enemy by use of force. (In the Ramayana) Rama killed Ravana in a tumultuous fight and relieved Sita. (In the Mahabharata) Krishna killed Kansa to end his wickedness; and Arjuna had to fight and slay quite a number of his friends and relations, including the revered Bhishma, because the latter was on the side of the aggressor. It is my firm belief that in dubbing Rama, Krishna and Arjuna as guilty of violence, the Mahatma betrayed the total ignorance of the springs of human action. In more recent history, it was the heroic fight put up by Chhatrapati Shivaji that first checked and eventually destroyed the Muslim tyranny in India. It was absolutely essential for Shivaji to overpower and kill an aggressive Afzal Khan, failing which he would have lost his own life. In condemning history's towering warriors like Shivaji, Rana Pratap and Guru Govind Singh as misguided patriots, Gandhi has merely exposed his self-conceit.

He was, paradoxical, as it may appear, a violent pacifist who brought untold calamities on the country in the name of truth and non-violence, while Rana Pratap, Shivaji and the Guru will remain enshrined in the hearts of their countrymen forever for the freedom they brought to them. The accumulating provocation of thirty-two years, culminating in his last pro-Muslim fast, at last goaded me to the conclusion that the existence of Gandhi should be brought to an end immediately. Gandhi had done very good work in South Africa to uphold the rights and well being of the Indian community there.

But when he finally returned to India, he developed a subjective mentality under which he alone was to be the final judge of what was right or wrong. If the country wanted his leadership, it had to accept his infallibility; if it did not, he would stand aloof from the Congress and carry on in his own way. Against such an attitude there can be no halfway house. Either Congress had to surrender its will to his and had to be content with playing second fiddle to all his eccentricity, whimsicality, metaphysics and primitive vision, or it had to carry on without him. He alone was the judge of everyone and everything; he was the master brain guiding the Civil Disobedience movement; no other could know the technique of that movement. He alone knew when to begin it and when to withdraw it. The movement might succeed or fail, but that could make no difference to the Mahatma's infallibility. 'A Satyagrahi can never fail' was his formula for his own infallibility and nobody except himself knew what a Satyagrahi is.

Thus the Mahatma became the judge and the jury in his own case. These childish insanities and obstinacies, coupled with a most severe austerity of life, ceaseless work and lofty character made Gandhi formidable and irresistible. Many people thought that his policies were irrational, but they had either to withdraw from the Congress or place their intelligence at his feet to do with as he liked. In a position of such absolute irresponsibility, Gandhi was guilty of blunder after blunder, failure after failure, and disaster after disaster. Gandhi's pro-Muslim policy is blatantly illustrated in his perverse attitude on the question of the national language of India. It is quite obvious that Hindi has the most prior claim to be accepted as the premier language.

In the beginning of his career in India, Gandhi gave a great impetus to Hindi, but as he found that the Muslims did not like it, he became a champion of what is called Hindustani. Everybody in India knows that there is no language in India called Hindustani; it has no grammar; it has no vocabulary. It is a mere dialect; it is spoken, not written. It is a tongue and a crossbreed between Hindi and Urdu, and not even the Mahatma's sophistry could make it popular. But in his desire to please the Muslims he insisted that Hindustani alone should be the national language of India. His blind followers, of course, supported him and the so-called hybrid language began to be used. The charm and the purity of the Hindi language were to be prostituted to please the Muslims. All his experiments were at the expense of the Hindus.

From August 1946 onwards, the private armies of the Muslim League began a massacre of Hindus. The then Viceroy, Lord Wavell, though distressed at what was happening, would not use his powers under the Government of India Act of 1935 to prevent the rape, murder and arson. The Hindu blood began to flow from Bengal to Karachi with little retaliation by the Hindus. The Interim Government formed in September was sabotaged by its Muslim League members right from its inception, but the more they became disloyal and treasonable to the government of which they were a part, the greater was Gandhi's infatuation for them.

Lord Wavell had to resign as he could not bring about a settlement and was succeeded by Lord Mountbatten. King Stork followed King Log. The Congress, which had boasted of its nationalism and secularism, secretly accepted Pakistan literally at the point of the bayonet and abjectly surrendered to Jinnah. India was vivisected and one-third of the Indian Territory became foreign land to us from 15 August 1947. Lord Mountbatten came to be described in the Congress circles as the greatest Viceroy and Governor-General this country ever had.

The official date for the handing over of power was fixed for June 30, 1948, but Mountbatten with his ruthless surgery gave us a gift of vivisected India ten months in advance. This is what Gandhi had achieved after thirty years of undisputed dictatorship and this is what the Congress party calls 'freedom' and 'peaceful transfer of power'. The Hindu-Muslim unity bubble was finally burst and a theocratic state was established with the consent of Nehru and his crowd and they have called it 'freedom won by them with sacrifice' - whose sacrifice? When top leaders of Congress, with the consent of Gandhi, divided and tore the country - which we considered a deity of worship - my mind was filled with direful anger.

One of the conditions imposed by Gandhi for his breaking of the fast related to the mosques in Delhi occupied by the Hindu refugees. But when Hindus in Pakistan were subjected to violent attacks he did not so much as utter a single word to protest and censure the Pakistan Government or the Muslims concerned. Gandhi was shrewd enough to know that while undertaking a fast unto death, had he imposed some conditions on the Muslims in Pakistan, here would have been found hardly any Muslims who could have shown some grief if the fast had ended in his death. It was for this reason that he purposely avoided imposing any conditions on the Muslims.

He was fully aware from past experience that Jinnah was not at all perturbed or influenced by his fast and the Muslim League hardly attached any value to the inner voice of Gandhi. Gandhi is being referred to as the Father of the Nation. But if that is so, he has failed in his paternal duty in as much he has acted very treacherously to the nation by his consenting to the partitioning of it. I stoutly maintain that Gandhi has failed in his duty. He has proved to be the Father of Pakistan. His inner-voice, his spiritual power, his doctrine of non-violence of which so much is made of, all crumbled against Jinnah's iron will and proved to be powerless.

Briefly speaking, I thought to myself and foresaw that I shall be totally ruined, and the only thing I could expect from the people would be nothing but hatred and that I shall have lost all my honour, even more valuable than my life, if I were to kill Gandhiji. But at the same time I thought that the Indian politics in the absence of Gandhiji would surely be practical, able to retaliate and would be powerful with the armed forces. No doubt, my own future would be totally ruined, but the nation would be saved from the inroads of Pakistan. People may even call me or dub me as devoid of any sense or foolish, but the nation would be free to follow the course founded on the reason, which I consider necessary for sound nation-building.

After having fully considered the question, I took the final decision in the matter, but I did not speak about it to anyone whatsoever. I took courage in both my hands and I did fire the shots at Gandhiji on 30th January 1948, on the prayer-grounds in Birla House. I do say that my shots were fired at the person whose policy and action had brought rack and ruin and destruction to millions of Hindus. There was no legal machinery by which such an offender could be brought to book and for this reason I fired those fatal shots. I bear no ill will towards anyone individually, but I do say that I had no respect for the present government owing to their policy, which was unfairly favourable towards the Muslims. But at the same time I could clearly see that the policy was entirely due to the presence of Gandhi.

I have to say with great regret that Prime Minister Nehru quite forgets that his preaching and deeds are at times at variance with each other when he talks about India as a secular state in season and out of season, because it is significant to note that Nehru has played a leading role in the theocratic state of Pakistan, and his job was made easier by Gandhi's persistent policy of appeasement towards the Muslims. I now stand before the court to accept the full share of my responsibility for what I have done and the judge would, of course, pass against me such orders of sentence as may be considered proper. But I would like to add that I do not desire any mercy to be shown to me, nor do I wish that anyone should beg for mercy on my behalf.

My confidence about the moral side of my action has not been shaken even by the criticism levelled against it on all sides. I have no doubt that honest writers of history will weigh my act and find the true value thereof someday in future."

Nathuram Godse was hanged a year later, on 15 November 1949; as per his last wishes, his family and followers have preserved his ashes for immersion in the Indus River of a re-united India.

❑

Who freed India?

Mahatama Gandhi or Subhash Chandra Bose?

While the declassification of the Netaji files has sparked off a massive debate on the need to rewrite modern Indian history, Netaji scholar and military historian General GD Bakshi claims that former British prime minister Clement Atlee said the role played by Netaji's Indian National Army was paramount in India being granted Independence, while the non-violent movement led by Gandhi was dismissed as having had minimal effect.

In the book, Bakshi cites a conversation between the then British PM Sir Attlee and then Governor of West Bengal Justice PB Chakraborty. The conversation is placed in 1956 when Attlee- the leader of Labour Party and the British premier who had signed the decision to grant Independence to India-had come to India and stayed in Kolkata as Chakraborty's guest.

Letter from the Chief Justice

Chakraborty, who was then the Chief Justice of the Calcutta High Court and was serving as the acting

Governor of West Bengal, had written a letter to the publisher of RC Majumdar's book, *A History of Bengal*, in which he wrote: "When I was acting governor, Lord Attlee, who had given us Independence by withdrawing British rule from India, spent two days in the governor's palace at Calcutta during his tour of India. At that time I had a prolonged discussion with him regarding the real factors that had led the British to quit India."

"My direct question to Attlee was that since Gandhi's Quit India Movement had tapered off quite some time ago and in 1947 no such new compelling situation had arisen that would necessitate a hasty British departure, why did they had to leave?"

"In his reply Attlee cited several reasons, the main among them being the erosion of loyalty to the British crown among the Indian Army and Navy personnel as a result of the military activities of Netaji," Chakraborty said.

"Toward the end of our discussion I asked Attlee what was the extent of Gandhi's influence upon the British decision to leave India. Hearing this question, Attlee's lips became twisted in a sarcastic smile as he slowly chewed out the word, 'm-i-n-i-m-a-l'," Chakraborty added. This startling conversation was first published by the Institute of Historical Review by author Ranjan Borra in 1982, in his piece on Subhas Chandra Bose, the Indian National Army and the war of India's liberation.

To understand the significance of Attlee's assertion, we have to go back in time to 1945. The Second World War had ended. The allied powers, led by Britain and the United States, had won. The Axis powers led by Hitler's Germany had been vanquished. The victors wanted to impose justice on the defeated armies. In India, officers of

Netaji Bose's Indian National Army were put on trial for treason, torture, murder. This series of court martials, came to be known as the Red Fort Trials.

Indian Soldiers' mutiny

Indians serving in the British armed forces were inflamed by the Red Fort Trials. In February 1946, almost 20,000 sailors of the Royal Indian Navy serving on 78 ships mutinied against the Empire. They went around Mumbai with portraits of Netaji and forced the British to shout Jai Hind and other INA slogans. The rebels brought down the Union Jack on their ships and refused to obey their British masters. This mutiny was followed by similar rebellions in the Royal Indian Air Force and also in the British Indian Army units in Jabalpur. The British were terrified. After the Second World War, 2.5 million Indian soldiers were being de-commissioned from the British Army.

Military intelligence reports in 1946 indicated that the Indian soldiers were inflamed and could not be relied upon to obey their British officers. There were only 40,000 British troops in India at the time. Most were eager to go home and in no mood to fight the 2.5 million battle hardened Indian soldiers, who were being de-mobilised. It is under these circumstances that the British decided to grant Independence to India.

The time has come to revisit modern Indian history and acknowledge the immense contribution of Netaji in helping India win its freedom.

Reference :

1. A History of Bengal *by* R.C. Majumdar
2. Bose : An Indian Samurai (Netaji and INA) A Military Assessment *by* Major General G. D. Bakshi

Photographs of the Event

Viceroy's House: The real story behind the partition of India and why Lord Mountbatten was wrongly vilified.

Mr. Jinha and Mahatama Gandhi in a happy mood.

Convicts of Gandhiji's Assassination in the Court-room

The Partition of India: A tale of violation of women's rights

Sept. 19, 1947: Muslim refugees sit on the roof of an over-crowded coach during partition (from Delhi to Lahore)

During partition, Hindu refugees sit on the roof of an overcrowded coaches form Lahore to Delhi.

The Agony of Partition (under non-violence freedom struggle of India lead by Mahatma Gandhi).

Around One lakh innocent people were killed and one million people became homeless during the Partition violence.

Vultures eating dead-bodies

Innocent victims of partition

The Survivors of the Partion of India & Refugee Camp behind

मैंने गांधी वध क्यों किया?
नाथुराम गोडसे
Rs. 175.00

बन्दी जीवन
शचीन्द्रनाथ सान्याल
सम्पूर्ण
Rs. 175.00

क्रांतिवीर
चंद्रशेखर आज़ाद
और उनके गद्दार साथी
Rs. 110.00

भगतसिंह
एक ज्वलन्त इतिहास
हंसराज रहबर
Rs 110.00

गाँधी बेनक़ाब
Rs. 150.00
हंसराज रहबर

हंसराज रहबर
नेहरू बेनकाब
Rs. 100.00

योद्धा संन्यासी
विवेकानंद
हंसराज रहबर
Rs. 150.00

राष्ट्र-नायक
गुरु गोविन्द सिंह
हंसराज 'रहबर'
Rs. 100.00

ब्रिटेन में भारतीय क्रांतिकारी
शहीद मदनलाल ढींगरा
एवं
शहीद सरदार ऊधम सिंह
पंडित सत्यनारायण शर्मा
Rs. 100.00

पहला किशोर क्रांतिकारी
खुदीराम बोस
Rs. 90.00

क्रान्तिकारी आन्दोलन
कुछ अधखुले पन्ने
Rs. 90.00
धर्मेन्द्र गौड़

मैं अंग्रेजों का जासूस था
धर्मेन्द्र गौड़
Rs. 110.00